Praise for *Read The Book*

With wisdom beyond her years, Stephanie A. Anderson continually proves time and time again that she does indeed live what she believes! A woman who wears many hats as a wife, mother and sister- she also lives beyond her personal world by wearing several more- leader, counselor, pastor and now, author. As an integral part of our Mannahouse family, she literally lives her life as an open book, blogging the real life struggles, emotions and relational obstacles we all face behind closed doors.

In Read the Book Stephanie communicates, with great clarity and practical insight, why we need the truth of the Bible and she gives practical steps in each chapter to help us see change in our lives. She offers up the simple, yet truly profound, gift of knowing we aren't alone on this journey. If you are looking for a book to help you in your walk with God, then look no further; this is the book for you. We're certain you'll enjoy her real and relatable stories which lead to her deeply personal revelations of discovery. Stephanie is a treasure to our family, and we're certain she'll be equally as valuable to yours. Enjoy the journey!
— Marc & Susan Estes; lead pastors, Mannahouse, Portland, Oregon

Stephanie's willingness to share her personal journey to articulate how alive and active God and His Word are in our lives is compelling. You will find yourself receiving honesty and hope, discipline and desire all in one masterfully written book. Highly recommend for one just beginning their walk with Jesus or one who has been in a relationship with Him for years. There is a breath of fresh air within the pages and practical tips to apply the Bible as a guiding force in your daily decisions.
— Raydeane Owens, co-lead pastor, Heart of the City, Coeur d'Alene, Idaho, contributor, Live Well Magazine CDA,

Some say 'advice is cheap' and that can be true. However, in my journey I have often found it to be the opposite. My life has been guided and blessed by wise input from people I trust. I have learned to be open to people who sincerely pursue truth, live the advice they give and genuinely have my best interest in mind. Here, I would like to recommend this book from Stephanie, as it comes from an honest life and heart that is passionately desiring to please God and help others. You will feel like you are sitting down at coffee with a wise friend who has prepared helpful thoughts just for you. She will bless you with practical wisdom springing from her life journey. As a witness to much of her life, I can say that this is valuable advice you can trust.
— Ken Malmin; dean and professor of theology, Portland Bible College, director, Academic Counsel for Educational Accountability Professionals Association

D1478213

Author Stephanie Anderson has written an intelligent instructional, challenging, and encouraging book that offers its readers rich insights into the benefits of reading and applying the Word of God. While it is filled with tweetable tweets and quotable quotes, it is very practical and applicable to one's daily life. The reader of this great book will walk away inspired, informed, and motivated to Read the Book and "Live Effectively."
— Glenda Malmin; dean of woman, Portland Bible College, professor of theology, author of Woman You Are Called and Anointed

Stephanie Anderson's Read the Book: One Way to Live Effectively is a beautiful roadmap for those longing to fall in love with the Word of God. Her passion for the veracity and hope contained within it is evident on every page of this book and has clearly been drawn from deep wells of study and experience. If you are looking to re-new your relationship with the power and wonder of the Bible, Read the Book is the perfect place to start.
— Bo Stern, teaching pastor, West Side Church, Bend, Oregon, founder, She.ology

It's rare in our fast-paced culture to sit down with a trusted and experienced guide who can navigate us through a learning curve. Stephanie's love for the Bible and years of gleaning its truths are a gift for anyone who's newer to their understanding of Scrip-ture. Imagine yourself sitting across from her at a local coffee shop and lean in as she pours out her wisdom. You'll love her stories, her insight, and the conversational feel of Read the Book!
— Jamie Schulz, co-lead pastor, Sun City Church, Spokane, Washington, founder, We CoLead

Stephanie's passion for the Word of God shines through in this book. As you read, you can't help but have some of her passion rub off! Full of practical recommenda-tions, helpful illustrations and personal testimonies, it's sure to take your hunger for the Bible to new places as you dig in and Read the Book. Whether you are newer to the scriptures or a life-long student of the Bible, this book is helpful and inspiring.
— Danny Schulz, co-lead pastor, Sun City Church, Spokane, Washington, founder, We CoLead

Read the Book is a strong reflection of the author Stephanie. It is passionate, heart-felt and practical with great stories. A preachers's kid, Stephanie knows the Bible and loves the Word but also understands the challenges and pitfalls. Let this book stir you in a new desire to explore this treasure chest - called the Bible.
— Rachel Hickson, founder, Heartcry For Change, Oxford, UK

I can't help but notice that Stephanie's writing gives the easy, warm feeling of a coffee date with a friend. Her words are encouraging, uplifting, and truly inspiring - you'll finish each chapter wanting to pursue the presence of God in bigger, more intimate ways. Throughout the book, Stephanie gives wise, practical guidance that is manageable in the face of a busy day-to-day routine. I'd recommend this book to anyone wanting to go deeper in their relationship with God - from the new believer desperately seeking more of God's presence, to the wise in faith searching and longing for fresh revelation. To whoever picks it up, this book is for you, and it won't disappoint.
— Megan Rueda; marriage and family therapist associate, Private Psychological Services of North Texas, Colleyville, Texas

Christianity is basically simple. We try to over complicate things by putting our faith in the wrong things. The life of the believer involves believing what God says, trusting that the Bible is truly God's word to us, seeking to know the truth and, most importantly, walking out that truth in our lives. In this book Stephanie takes us on a personal journey and helps us to discover a new love for the Word and practical tips to bringing it into a more significant place in our day-to-day lives. She also helps us to hear God's voice through the pages of the Bible. Her book is simple, personal and profound all that the same time. You will be blessed if you follow the prescription for success found in its pages.
— Bill Shiedler, executive director, Church Leadership Resources

READ THE BOOK

READ THE BOOK

One Way to Live Effectively

Stephanie A. Anderson

ISBN: 978-1-7331892-0-0

Cover design: Kristen Ingebretson

Cover image: Federico X. Serrano

Interior Layout: Stephanie Anderson

Printed in the United States of America
23 22 21 20 19 — 5 4 3 2 1

I dedicate this book to my children

Boston and Brecken

with the prayer that you would be skilled in the Word
and always pursue Jesus.

"God never negotiates with men. Jesus Christ's death on the cross put an end to any kind of negotiations. It is now Christ or nothing. It is now God's Word in its entirety or nothing." —A.Z. Tozer, *God's Power for Your Life: How the Holy Spirit Transforms You Through God's Word*

Contents

Foreword

In many ways Stephanie has been working her entire life to write this book. She isn't a fair-weather christian who reads her Bible only when things are good or bad like many of us do. From the moment I met her in a prayer circle I knew she was a passionate follower of Jesus. You could see this was true by looking at her Bible. She was seventeen years old and her Bible looked like it had belonged to an old lady who was dedicated to that church for years. The front cover was barely attached, pages missing and more scriptures were highlighted and underlined than were not. She loved her Bible and not just for status or as a token of her faith, but she longed to know its truths, to let them shape her, change her and to communicate what God was speaking to anyone that would listen.

For the next several years as our relationship would form it was her leadership and love for God's Word, applying practically and living principally, that was so attractive to me. Don't get me wrong, she's beautiful on the outside too, but her love for Jesus and His Word sealed the deal for me. Throughout our marriage I have seen her daily lean on the truths found in scripture, in parenting, loving the lost, and continually growing in her own walk with the Lord. Stephanie always wants what she learns from God's word to shape her.

Many people tend to learn about life through trial and error. However, Stephanie might be the most driven person I've ever met. I mean, who else sits down to watch a movie after a long day and also has their laptop out to research and learning something at the same time. That's where you will find Stephanie almost every day and it's almost always around a topic she is writing on for an upcoming blog post or about some passage of scripture she is wrapping her mind around personally. She has given herself to the study of the Word and how that in turn can help her and those she pastors.

Read the Book is not just a clever title but the first of many practical and easily applicable steps in this book. Stephanie has taken the daunting task of explaining the importance of reading the Bible and applying its principals and is reshaping the conversation making it a simple coffee shop mentoring moment. Stephanie and I are both millennials and we have realized that our generation is running from organized religion in masses. One of the many reasons I believe this to be the case is because there isn't a proper understanding of what Christianity is. We tend to forget that our walk with the Lord isn't about what we can do for God, rather it's about what God has already done for us. *Read the Book* helps people understand that God didn't give us His Word as something to be endured or a weapon to be used against other people, but a guide to help us navigate our journey through life. God does not want us to just barely get by but to live victoriously on a daily basis.

My hope for you is that as you will read this book and allow the personal stories to draw you in and show you that there is, for every situation we face, a scripture that can be used to help better navigate that part of our lives. Stephanie is just like everyone else, the only difference might be that through trials, triumphs and tragedies she has remained devoted to the *Read The Book* and live its truths. God bless and enjoy!

Trevin Anderson
Husband and Staff Pastor at Mannahouse

Preface

During my childhood I collected different awards as incentives for bringing my Precious Moments Bible to Kingdom Kids on Sundays. I was a pastor's kid and was becoming familiar with the voice of God. (Becoming familiar with God's voice doesn't mean it is easy to trust it; it just means I had learned to hear it.) I was so fortunate to be raised in a family and church where the members love the Word of God and do their best to understand it and live by it.

While I was in high school my youth pastor taught a series on the Bible. I don't remember the title or the branding of his presentation, but I do know that as I sat in the front row doing math homework (which is probably why I don't remember much), seeds were being planted in my heart—seeds of passion for the Word. To this day I believe that series of messages was just for me. It stirred a hunger in me to know the content found on the pages of my Bible. Every Wednesday I looked forward to Gen Church, our church's high-school student gathering, as I wanted to hear and know more about the Bible. I remember three things from that series:

1. About forty different authors wrote the Bible. They lived different lifestyles, had different family structures and educational backgrounds, and held different economic and political points of view. This group of writers was a diverse bunch! Yet there is no error or contradiction in the Bible between them because they were all inspired by God. I learned that if some-

thing in the Bible doesn't seem to make sense or appears to show contradiction, it's because I was reading with my personal worldview as the filter. The idea of team-writing and context principle still challenge and inspire me today. (Context principle comes from the idea that one statement is part of a larger message and can't stand alone; otherwise, the statement loses its full meaning.) The fact that it took upwards of 1,500 years to write the Bible is also an incredible sign that God was involved in the process.

2. The Bible contains sixty-six separate books. Each of them is inspired by God and make up the Canon, which means "measure" in the Greek language.[1] In high school, I learned the Bible should be the standard by which I measure my life.

3. Throughout history, and still today, there has been opposition to the Bible. The Good Book has survived burnings, banishment in certain countries and institutions, and movements led by deep hostility toward the authority of its pages. There has never been a more influential book than the Bible. God's Word has prevailed throughout history. Think about it: people hate Bible believers. In the United States Bible readings were banned in public schools in 1963,[2] and people all over the world believe only portions of the Bible because they view it as hard to understand. But Truth is the same yesterday, today, and forever. God's Word is still here. God's ability to cover and protect His message, regardless of the opposition it has faced, proves His sovereignty. God is always in control; and His Word will never be useless, will always exist, and will always produce results (Isaiah 55:11).

Looking at past messages I have taught since I was a teenager, I notice a common thread: They all point to the

Word. What is the "Word"? "The Word" is another way of referring to the Bible.

On July 11, 2004 my church's children's pastor trusted me with the Sunday morning kid's ministry pulpit while he was away on vacation. I was seventeen years old, and I was so nervous about sharing. My notes were in twenty-point font, and on both sides of the page I had written, "Speak slow" and "Breathe." The topic that day is still relevant today, and I want to share with you the points from that message:

- God has a word for everyone.
- God has a word for every day.
- Every word has (requires) a response.
- Every word has (includes) instructions.
- I can get every word God has for me.

On August 22nd of that same year I had the privilege of preaching in the junior-high class. The topic? "Taking Over the World for Jesus." (That's a totally realistic goal for a seventeen-year-old with big dreams, right? Very little has changed—well, except my age.) Here are the main points of that day's message:

1. What does it take to take over the world?
Faith.

2. What is faith?
"Faith is the assurance (title deed, confirmation) of things hoped for (divinely guaranteed), and the evidence of things not seen [the conviction of their reality—faith comprehends as fact what cannot be experienced by the physical

senses]." (Hebrews 11:1 AMP) and "Firm belief in something for which there is no proof."[3]

3. How do we get faith?
We get faith by reading the Bible, and believing its content, and by listening to God. It's possible to read and still not believe it. (Romans 10:17)

4. What do we do with faith?
"Therefore we also, since we are surrounded by so great a cloud of witnesses, let us lay aside every weight, and the sin which so easily ensnares us, and let us run with endurance the race that is set before us." (Hebrews 12:1)

5. How do we run the race?
"Looking unto Jesus, the author and finisher of our faith." (Hebrews 12:2)

6. What is practical? (Yes! I actually asked this question, even as a teen.)
Inviting people to church and telling people about Jesus Christ. (Tell them His story.)

7. God has called you to take over the world, your world, by faith, which comes by hearing the Word and looking to Jesus.

To this day, I believe these thoughts are true, but as I have grown up I have realized the Bible does not communicate to me how to make decisions for a fulfilling life in the way I want to be communicated to. I don't always find a practical list of things to do so that I am able to live an effective, successful, and meaningful life. In the pages of this book I begin to break down the process of understanding how the Bible is a tool that is both powerful and practical for every day choices. I think about my country and my generation across the world, and I want them to learn the content of the Bible; and be inspired to live a life that matches what they understand.

I am not writing this book because I have mastered understanding the Bible, but because I am looking at what is in my hands (Exodus 4:2) and asking, "What can I do to further spread the Gospel?" I believe part of spreading the Gospel is helping people understand it. If the Bible is the Gospel story, understanding the Bible is key. I am believing as you read this book a hunger to discover the Word and understand how it is relevant to your life today will be ignited.

Acknowledgments

Mr. Trevin Anderson: Thank you for inspiring me to be me; nothing more and nothing less. Also, for taking care of the loads of laundry and the sink full of dirty dishes as I have been "mom-ing" all day and writing all night. I'm grateful. I love you honey!

Boston and Brecken: My darlings, you have motivated me to face my fears and inspired me to follow Jesus better. I couldn't be more proud of you. I love you boys!

Angie Riesterer: I am so grateful for the time and care you spent editing the first draft of my first book. Thank you for being brave enough to be the first pair of eyes on this project and the seed of a dream. Your support means the world to me.

Julie Duncan: Thank you so much for answering all of my book questions, and for geeking out with me about the creation of a book and all that it entails. You have a wealth of knowledge about the publishing world and have so kindly shared and encouraged me along the way. I am so grateful.

Glenda Malmin: I look forward to every mentoring moment we share. I am so fortunate to be mentored and challenged by you. Thank you for your example as a woman in the ministry and specifically for the time and wisdom you have invested into my life as a wife, mom, and minister. You have truly shaped my story by sharing yours.

Steve & Taunia Meistrell: Mom and Dad, you have shaped me from the moment I was born. I am grateful for both of you. Thank you for everything you have done to set me up for a great relationship with Jesus and a great life. I love you both very much!

Powerful and Practical

In April 2016, in Kumamoto, Japan, a middle-aged man opened the passenger-side door to his car for his wife to get in. He closed the door and proceeded to walk around to the driver's side. Just before getting inside the car, he looked around —at his home and property—and took a deep breath; then he sat down inside the car and closed the door. It was a quiet moment with only a loud sigh in the middle of the unknown. On his wife's lap was a blanket, and next to her head was the pillow she rested on, but there was no plan to travel anywhere. They were sleeping in their car because they felt ultimately this was the safest place for them to sleep that night.

Just two days before Kumamoto had experienced an earthquake with a magnitude of 6.9 on the intensity scale; and though their house was still standing, they had a feeling something wasn't right. In the wee hours of the next morning, at about 1:25 a.m., the main earthquake at a magnitude of 7.3 shook Kumamoto, which meant the previous earthquake had been a foreshock of what was to come. Parents were in pain seeing the fear in their children's eyes. Children were upset seeing their parents so stressed. Buildings collapsed completely, roads split, thousands were injured, and dozens of lives were lost. The couple sleeping in their car woke up in the middle of the earthquake only to watch their home implode right in front of them. Everything was destroyed. Well almost; they still had each other.

A year later, my husband had the privilege of meeting this man, hearing his story, and seeing the damage that still existed from the earthquake.

Just four days after the 2016 earthquakes, a church in Kumamoto formed the Kyushu Christ Disaster Relief Center.[1] Since that time hundreds of groups from all over the world have partnered with this center by either giving money, sending supplies, or sending teams to assist in the cleanup and rebuilding of the Kumamoto Prefecture and the surrounding district. In 2017, about fifteen months after the founding of the relief center, my husband, Trevin, led a short-term mission trip to partner with the relief center. During the time spent there, the team heard stories of loss and stories of provision, and they worked hard to accomplish their assignments with care and excellence. Yet, even as rebuilding was taking place, the mission team watched as Typhoon Noru developed along the Pacific and threatened Japan. South Osaka, where the team was stationed, was in the direct path of this storm.

I was at home in Portland, Oregon, with our two little boys, ages one and six, knowing that while my husband was helping others to rebuild from a previous disaster, another was possibly on its way. My mom drove seven hours from Idaho to stay with us while Trevin was out of the country. I found myself thinking about storms, recovering from pain, living in ruins and brokenness, and how we can't control when "storms" hit, but we can trust God during them. Thankfully, Noru settled down from a Category 5 to a Category 1 by the time it hit Japan; and though the rainfall from this storm was immense, the people there were able to live through what had to have felt like the longest three days ever. I was relieved to know that our team moved south before the storm made landfall and were safe to continue their work of bringing hope to the people of Japan.

This trip Trevin took to Japan was the "final thread" to a long list of thoughts I've had since my youth—thoughts that have woven together to confirm how I have decided to live the rest of my life. When Trevin came home I listened to his stories about the trip, and he said something that answered questions I have had for awhile now and quieted the unsettled feeling I was having as I thought more about the concept of making decisions based on a calling and living a Spirit-led life. I had come to know Jesus based on my background—a white American Christian culture—and yet my spirit was leading me in a different direction. Trevin shared with me a perspective that made my commitment to Christ richer, enhanced my love for the Word, and changed how I engage and care for people.

I am a pastor and a pastor's wife who grew up as a pastor's kid. I attended a Bible college; and before that, I led Bible studies at the public junior high and high school I attended. I made a list of the fourteen friends I wanted to bring to church in high school and checked off their names as they began their own journeys with the Lord. I served at church events and studied how our country was formed on Christianity. Later, I wrote curriculums for children's camps and Sunday morning programs, and I have taught Christian theology to adults. I went to Christian concerts and had the "JC - Jesus Pieces"

Calvin Klein knock-off T-shirt. I was raised being asked "What would Jesus do?" and having to find the answer, rather than laugh at this mass-produced phrase that stirred many emotionally but motivated only some. I have been so fortunate to have parents and leaders in my life who led me to love the Lord and encouraged my love for people. I was taught a lot and I knew a lot; I was (and still am) so blessed. However, I still struggled because I knew something was missing; something was unsettled and questions were unanswered. I knew I needed answers, not just for me, but for my kids, their kids, and others who want to live powerful lives but struggle to understand how to do so practically. I, myself, am still searching, but this book contains what I've learned so far.

Enough about Me—What Did Trevin Say?

I have observed that anytime someone leaves the United States to serve people in another country, that specific person comes home with a changed life. Trevin was no exception, and the Japanese values made an impact on him. Knowing this, I was so excited to extend my love to Japan as my best friend left to serve and build (something he loves to do!). When Trevin returned home, he began talking about the Japanese culture and about how it affected the culture of the churches in Japan. I remember joking, should we move to Japan? I felt as if we shared a lot of the same values as the community he spent time with. Trevin talked about their families, about how the parents love and invest in their children, the cleanliness of the streets in the suburbs, the honor/shame culture, and, of course, the beautiful churches the team had the privilege of serving. Then he said something that connected the dots for me regarding how our daily choices affect our destiny. I felt as if I was working on a puzzle with the right piece in my hand, and it just needed to be flipped around to fit correctly. He said this:

> They serve their church because of how great God is. Not because it is their job, because it isn't. Different groups would volunteer to take turns over the different weekends caring for the maintenance and cleanliness of their facility. They don't serve God because of what God or the church can do for them. They don't serve God because they have some special gift to contribute to their community. They serve the church and the people because of who God is and how that understanding of His greatness dictates their choices in life. They serve because they understand that in serving people, they are serving God.

Their actions were out of obedience, loyalty, and dependence on the One who is in control of their lives. They live in surrender to a Lord. The Lord. This may sound obvious, but it's not, it's really not, at least not here in the U.S. In my beloved country, we encourage people to join a local church because of what the church does for them; we promise benefits to unconfirmed members, and we lose our young at the same time due to a lack of experiencing the life-changing power of God's love. It's heartbreaking.

Since my husband has taken this trip to Japan, we have discussed frequently the difference between Jesus being our "Savior" and Jesus being our "Lord." I didn't grow up in a monarchy type of government, so having a king that I served or represented wasn't a lifestyle during my childhood. My choices weren't decided for me ahead of time. I wasn't raised in a theocracy, where priests were the governmental rule, guiding people to know God and live by His standards. The more I studied, the clearer the concept of Lordship and surrender became. Jesus was my Lord and Savior; yet so often I only resourced Jesus as my Savior, instead of submitting my thoughts and daily choices to Christ as my Lord. I asked myself, "What choices am I making, and how does that reflect Christianity?" Thus my journey to discover more of what God desired from me was locked in. I have found my choices were decided for me ahead of time. Jesus said, "Love God and love people." (Mark 12:30-31, my paraphrase).

The book of Hebrews says Jesus is the pioneer and perfecter of our faith (12:2 NIV). He not only created a way, He perfected the way to live as a Christian. I have only lived one life. That is, this life of faith that I live I am currently living and learning to live, but Jesus has lived a life of faith, a perfect one; and as I surrender all the practical things (my actions and daily practices)[2] in my life to Him, the result is a powerful life. Yet living powerfully and effectively can't happen without knowing to whom I am surrendering my life. It's logical to think. "Why trust someone I don't know?" We learn to trust God as we get to know Him, and to know God we read the Bible.

God is Practical

I want to share some practical things I have learned about God. First, God is a very understandable and present God. He is not someone that we can't understand or someone with whom we can't connect. Even though there is always more to learn, and we can always grow in our understanding of Him, there are things He wants us to know about Him. Absolute truth exists, and we can be sure that He gave us that truth. He is available in the everyday, real life. He knows we need creativity to thrive and routine to sustain us day by day.

Another thing I learned is that God is an organized God. He created the world before creating the animals. Why? Order! To be more specific, if God created animals first, they would have floated in a space of nothingness without the right atmosphere and nutrients to flourish. God desires order in our lives as well. Order creates an atmosphere that we can settle into, so we can grow and flourish. Order is needed for the small, seemingly powerless decisions we make in our everyday lives, the practical things we do.

Have you ever heard the term success sequence? Success sequence basically means that when certain decisions are made and worked out in a specific order, your success in that area increases. The same is true with our lives. God is our Creator. He created all life, including the human race. So, if we want to have success and live effectively according to how He defined it, we must read his guidebook—the Bible.

The older I get (Am I actually claiming the word "old?"), the more I am learning that my role or existence as a Christian is very practical. Our God is a very practical God. He cares about our lives and our role in society. Learning these things gives me the confidence to live in the real world. His original design for humans includes our living a life of order.

Defining Power

When I was a little girl I would walk into my parents' room in the evening, after dinner was over and the dishes were cleaned, and I would find my mom sitting on her bed studying.

She wasn't finishing a degree or studying to preach; she was studying for her life and her heart. Studying was different back then. I remember life without the internet and studying without search engines in the palm of my hand (I guess I am claiming the word "old.")

Mom studied with a notebook, a dictionary, a Strong's Concordance, and other Bible study books, wide open with different colors of sticky notes as bookmarks. Lined up in a row would be pens, highlighters, and three-by-five note cards. The different colors represented different things she discovered: actions, attitudes, promises, and definitions. She would organize her thoughts or highlight answers to some of life's biggest questions, including how to deal with loss or why bad things happen to good people. Studying this way wasn't her way of practicing for events, or only for moments when she got to speak, it was a regular discipline in our home. Mom studied the Bible to apply it to her own life. In fact, she studied the fruits of the Spirit regularly. I didn't understand the importance of that until my late teens and my life was really in my control and I had to figure out for myself what was next.

So often I heard my mom pray, "Every promise in the book is mine" (2 Corinthians 1:20). After hearing her pray that over and over again, I wanted to know if every promise could be mine too. The primary definition of the word power is the "ability to act or produce an effect."[3] A secondary definition of the word power is "possession of control, authority, or influence over."[4] Nothing can ruin or weaken the power that is found within the pages of the Bible. In my life, I have also found that God's Word is not useless! It is powerful and practical! The Bible promises that if we act and make choices

8

based on what we are reading (and learning) about God, we can live a life that is effective and fulfilling.

Living powerfully is a choice. We can choose to live a life that is surrendered to God, who is all powerful, and allow His power to influence our everyday choices. Whether you grew up in church or you didn't, every promise in the Bible is available to you! I constantly remind myself that God is for me and not against me (Romans 8:31). God wants me to succeed! He has proven that He will never leave me nor forsake me (Joshua 1:5). He has never left my side, and nothing can separate me from His love (Romans 8:38-39).

To live effectively in the moment is to feel every emotion, think through every possibility, and get all the facts that you can; and, at the end of the day, to allow God's Word to guide our words and behaviors because power comes from our obedience to the Word.

Living a powerful life requires complete dependence on the One who is all-powerful for our daily choices and habits. (We'll cover this in the next chapter.) But, before turning the page, consider the decisions you will need to make in the next few years, and the choices you most likely didn't make but were made for you at one time—choices that you may make for someone else in the future. These are the practical decisions you have to live through. Understand this: you can make decisions confidently based on the powerful Word of God. Here are some examples:

Choices You Most Likely Didn't Make

• Living Arrangements: shelter, apartment, studio, shared house, townhouse, mansion

- Education: early childhood, elementary, middle school, and high school
- Natural Abilities: sports, music, technology, art, and so on
- Benefits and Pay: what your hard work earns
- Family Identity: how people see you due to the family you grew up in
- Family Traditions: the fun ones and the creepy old ones
- Family Struggles: abuse, debt, pain, and so on
- Mental, emotional, and physical responses to the environment we grew up in, both culturally and spiritually

Choices You Will Most Likely Get to Make

- Who to date
- Which colleges to apply for (most likely influenced by budget, goals, and culture)
- What substances and foods you put into your body and how much you exercise
- Job choice (You fill out the applications, right?)
- Debts and investments
- Who you have sex with
- Who you will marry
- Will you go to church? If so, which one?
- How many kids you will have (or at least try to have)?
- Your character: How you choose to act regardless of how family and the community has treated you and labeled you.

The Problem with Jesus, Our Lord and Savior

Jesus is Lord, and Jesus is Savior. These two truths that we hold as Christians give us power in our practical living. However, while I was growing up I had a problem: it was difficult for me to believe the things the Bible says about Jesus Christ are true. How can Jesus tell us to love our enemies? When He said that, didn't He know that America's enemies would be starving people and killing babies? And surely Jesus didn't mean I have to love the people who are causing problems in my personal life and especially those who post inconsiderate things online. If we misunderstand this and other truths in the Bible, it can be a hindrance in our daily lives.

When the Bible doesn't seem to "fit" my life, I've found the problem isn't that the Bible doesn't fit; the problem is that I don't understand the Bible in the way the Author intended. Plus, I am not living the way I was originally created to live. In fact, living that way doesn't even come naturally. So I can't even begin to understand the message of the Bible and see change in my life until I learn what it is actually saying. I live my life ineffectively until I discover the way it was originally meant to be. I must study Scripture with an idea, with curiosity, and ask questions. To show you what I mean, let's ask two basic questions and find the answers in the Bible: (1) Who is Jesus? and (2) What role does He have in my powerful and practical living? Romans 10:9 says "If you confess with your mouth the Lord Jesus and believe in your heart that God has raised Him from the dead, you will be saved." What we can discover from this scripture?

- Jesus is the Lord.
- Jesus died.
- God raised Jesus from the dead, so
- God is more powerful than death.
- Jesus is alive.

If we accept these short phrases as truth, our actions should change, and we can be spared from a life full of regrets. Thus, "you will be saved"! But how can we be saved from death? Death is real, and many people fear it more than anything else. But, what about living a life that is not worth living; being dead inside, without passion or a dream? God can save us from a life that isn't worth living.

Our confession, something else that is practical, and belief in Jesus can save us from living lives that are unintentional and unfulfilling. How often do we confess Christ instead of confessing our life experiences? How often do we compare our thoughts to the Bible's content and let the Bible have the last word? There are two things in Romans 10:9 that I want to highlight: Jesus is Lord and Jesus is Savior.

Jesus is Lord on His own; nothing we do makes Him a lord. However, we can surrender our choices to His plans and accept His ruling or Lordship. Then He becomes our Lord. What is a lord? A lord is someone who is the ruler or the expert in something.[1] We get to choose to surrender to Him by submitting our emotions and thoughts to what we are reading in the Bible about Him. (How often do we surrender our ideas?) Likewise, Jesus is a Savior, but He is not our Savior unless we recognize our need for Him. Jesus can only be our Savior if we confess our sins and accept His forgiveness. To say it another way, Jesus is the Savior, but if we don't ask Him to help us, He isn't our Savior. (How often do we ask for help?)

One definition of the word believe is "accept[ing] something as true, genuine, or real."[2] When we believe something to be true, our ideas, emotions, and choices will align with that truth. If your doctor tells you that you have three months to live unless you change your diet, would you change your diet? Of course you would because you believe the doctor. The concept is the same with belief in Jesus. So many individuals are walking around saying they "believe" in Jesus—He is their Lord and Savior—but they still walk around stuck, thinking sinful thoughts that affect their habits and choices, leading them to live through experiences they are ashamed of or have to apologize for later.

Our sinful thoughts effect our habits, and our habits effect our decisions, making us powerless and living without purpose. We are constantly taking Jesus as Savior for granted. He is the only one who has mastered holy living and is the expert at overcoming death. Rather than respecting Him for who He is, we take Him for granted and render Him powerless in our daily lives.

Through the years, as I have learned to trust the Bible, I have been released from others' opinions and lies that limited me. I thought my own logic would help me build a better life; but, in fact, only following Jesus the Lord leads me to a better life. In John 14:6 Jesus said, "I am the way, the truth, and the life." In order to know which way we should choose, in order to know what truth we should believe, and in order to know what life could be possible, we must get to know Jesus better. We should follow Christ instead of our logic and instead of our emotions. Jesus said in John 10:10, "I have come that they may have life, and that they may have it more abundantly." This is the truth.

You may find it difficult to believe that Jesus has that much influence over life and death because of your current situation or past. Let's consider the words of Paul the apostle: "I can do all things through Christ, who gives me strength" (Philippians 4:13). The Amplified Bible says, "I can do all things [which He has called me to do] through Him who strengthens and empowers me [to fulfill His purpose— I am self-sufficient in Christ's sufficiency; I am ready for anything and equal to anything through Him who infuses me with inner strength and confident peace.]"

Paul wrote this letter to Christians in Philippi. He was in prison, some say in a city called Ephesus, when he wrote these words about ten years after he visited Philippi. This was not the first time Paul had been imprisoned and bound by chains; his situation was nothing new. Paul was writing in a limited space and in unfriendly territory, yet he was able to find strength to write these life-changing words. He was in double confinement: prison and chains. No, wait, triple confinement: there was also a guard! Yet he still believed he was a free man. He understood that being limited physically didn't equal being limited spiritually because he served a limitless God.

Perhaps you feel limited in your potential at work because you don't have a car. Perhaps you feel limited in a relationship, however you are afraid of what might happen if you stand up for yourself. Physical limitations don't have to restrain you spiritually when you serve a limitless God. The truth is, you can find ways to act in these situations that can be effective and bring fulfillment. Our fulfillment should be found in obeying the Lord, rather than achieving a result or fairness in life we feel we should receive.

Paul wasn't above the law, but his God was above all limitations. Though Paul was in chains, he understood that God is the Ruler over all things and all people, including the chain-makers. This is an example of how studying a verse can make it powerful and personal to you. Instead of just wishing or praying you can be free from physical chains, you can trust that the Lord will sustain you in the "triple confinement" seasons of your life.

Do you remember about my mom studying the Bible at night? She studied for life, for this kind of perspective. When I think about the rough situations and the incredible opportunities that become available to me, and when I think about things I have learned from the Bible, that is what carries me through each decision. I love the clean pages in my Bible that are ready for me to scribble on as the Holy Spirit speaks, and the cover that isn't dented yet or discolored from a coffee cup. However, with the passing of time, I have been able to see that I always have access to this reality and influence anywhere.

And now, anywhere I take my phone I have access to studying the Word. I can look something up so quickly, and my time is saved. (Take care to notice if the websites and articles you view line up with the Bible instead of someone's experience or opinion. In the Appendix of this book, I share with you some of my favorite resources.)

You might be in a situation you can't change, but that doesn't mean God can't change the situation. Again, let's take our lead from Paul's experience. His power wasn't in his perspective or in his position; Paul's power was found in the person of Jesus Christ. This is so contrary to what is happening in our world today. Paul and his friend (also in chains) started singing and lifting up the name of Jesus, the Lord, who once again proved to be his Savior by breaking the chains that held them. As a result of this chain-breaking miracle, the guard saw Jesus reflected in Paul's hope despite his being chained. The guard became a believer, and his family did too! Our logic and knowledge of the truth are worthless until we genuinely believe it more than opinions, feelings, and experiences. If you want to use your voice, use it to lift up the name of Jesus, speak of God's greatness rather than someone else's perspective or position. Perhaps, like Paul, our trials are the best place to show the saving knowledge of Jesus Christ, our Lord.

Our chains aren't intended to keep us bound; they are so we can help others find Christ if we recognize the opportunity for it. Let's think of ourselves like Paul when he said in Philippians 1:13-14, "My chains are in Christ; and most of the brethren in the Lord, having become confident by my chains, are much more bold to speak the Word without fear." Consider this: as Christians we are chained for the purpose of honoring the Lord Jesus, regardless of our pain and discomfort.

Can I encourage you to look at your situation with the possibility that God can reveal His power through your struggle? I believe He has chosen you (like He chose Paul) and has allowed you to walk through difficult seasons so that others can grow in their faith as they see you stay committed to Jesus Christ, the Lord. Let's surrender to the Lord and watch Him act as Lord and Savior in and around us, for everyone!

Now let's look at Philippians 4:13 from another angle but still focus on how Jesus really has so much power in our lives, specifically releasing us from the wounds, lies and limitations of our past, by learning about Paul's audience and why he wrote this particular message to the Philippians.

Philippi was a Roman colony and a diverse city that benefitted from being loyal to Rome. Military soldiers were encouraged to retire there, preserving its loyalty. Let's sit here on this one fact.

Here is an example of the Bible being powerful and very practical! By studying behind the scenes of the Bible, I find confidence in making decisions by thinking about how the truths in the passage match my life now. I don't mean confidence as a feeling, but confidence as in a mental reassurance and peace in my soul beyond everything I know that is true. This is how "faith comes by hearing" (Romans 10:17). My life is different because what I believe to be true affects it.

What Did I Learn?

Here it is: retired soldiers were living in Philippi, assuring the city's loyalty to Rome, to take advantage of all its benefits. The soldiers weren't the majority of the population living there; however, their influence and loyalty to Rome was significant. Knowing that was the case prompts me to ask myself,

"In what areas of my life have I let one or two wrong things from the past dictate my everyday life in the present? What situation should be 'retired' but still affects the way I live? Maybe there are past lies, or possibly wounds from a difficult situation. We must recognize the strong voices from the past that are holding us back from following Jesus. Our identity comes from loyalty to Him instead of the lies or habits in our lives. If we are surrendered to Christ, these habits have to change also.

Lifting up the name of the Lord, in worship, as Paul did, opens the door for the power of the Holy Spirit to move in our lives. Lies have to melt in weakness, and chains have to break. In other words, we have the opportunity to change, as well as the grace and strength to change, by remaining surrendered to the one who transforms us over time—as we focus on the truth. So my question is this: How many of us are living with retired "soldiers" that keep us from advancing in levels of holiness? Holiness is being separated from those things so that God can be seen in us, which is His ultimate purpose for our lives.

Your past doesn't have to dictate your future. You don't have to be a byproduct of your environment. Is your past keeping you loyal to fear? To unforgiveness? To anything else that is sinful or unhealthy?

Even if we are in unfriendly or toxic situations, we must activate our faith and choose truth. Jesus is all-powerful, and He can give us the ability to live powerful lives as we trust Him in the practical spaces such as work, school, and family.

Believing the truth is important. No matter what chains are trying to hold you down or what "retired soldiers" are pressuring you to be loyal to the past—to something other than Jesus, the Lord of lords—no lie and no past have power over Him.

If you have prayed and asked Jesus to be your Lord and Savior, the past can stay in the past. You may need to change some habits, forgive someone, or talk with a counselor in order to "retire" the soldiers. But if you have accepted the incredible undeserved gift of salvation, you have the ability to live a powerful life starting now.

Salvation: Brings Order from the Inside-Out

God existed before the world, our little galaxy, and the entire expanse of the universe. This God expresses Himself in three ways: as the Father, as the Son, and as a Spirit: the Holy Spirit. God decided to create the universe and all its complexities, from the smallest atom in the bottom of the deepest ocean to the unending edges of the universe, and He still holds all of this in His sturdy hand. Not one thing happens that He does not know about.

After God created our galaxy and, specifically, Earth, He created two humans. These two humans were going to model for the rest of us how to live on this planet. The first human was a man named Adam. The second human created was a woman named Eve. They were not superhuman; they are normal people just like us who walked with God on the earth in a special place called the garden of Eden.

God gave Adam and Eve instructions for living in this garden. He gave them tasks as well, such as naming the animals, plants, and having children. God was their Lord, or King and He gave them the freedom to make their own choices while living on the earth. Still, every king has a kingdom, and the culture of his kingdom is distinct. Laws must be followed to stay within the boundaries and receive the benefits of the kingdom.

Here is where things get confusing. There was one tree in the garden that grew fruit—one tree from which God told Adam and Eve not to eat. Eve was deceived by what Satan, in the form of a serpent, told her, and she ate the fruit. Seeing that her disobedience didn't end her life immediately, she shared the fruit with Adam. Since I haven't had the opportunity to sit down and have coffee with Eve, I try putting myself in her shoes and considering this experience as if it were my own.

Eve may have been thinking about death in human terms, rather than according to Kingdom culture. God had given the humans control over their daily choices. The power of their decisions came from doing things the Lord's way; but in this case, they didn't do things His way. Kingdom culture is living the way God wants us to live, every day.

You see, just because they were the first humans and they knew God, it doesn't mean they understood everything about Him. Instead, they (and we) need to consider death in Kingdom terms. Life without God is a slow, physical death towards an eternal, spiritual death, which is a permanent experience filled with fear, pain, and the absence of the presence of God. Human nature, our fleshly nature, is in constant conflict with this holy God. Choosing to live based upon our natural tendencies is against God's will. This act of disobeying God's will is called sin. When Adam and Eve sinned, God moved them out of the garden, and they had to live a life that was distant from Him. God was still around and available to them, but they couldn't relate to Him in the same way, because God is holy (without sin) and they had become sinful.

God gave them new laws (boundaries) to help Adam and Eve live outside of the garden and still be able to know Him—

a new order. But these laws were difficult to keep, since the problem was inside of them, and laws only address outside actions. Outside actions don't change inside problems.

The same is true for us today—no one is perfect; no one has power over sin unless the person is holy (separated to God). In fact, Romans 3:23 says, "For all have sinned and fall short of the glory of God." Every one of us is wonderfully created by God (Psalm 139); but we are also born into a life of sin. We need another human to show us how to live this life. That is Jesus Christ, the expert. We are in need of a savior in order to be in right relationship with God and to overcome that sin. This Savior, this hero, this Lord, is Jesus! He is the Son of God. John 3:16 says "For God so loved the world that He gave His only begotten Son, that whoever believes in Him should not perish but have everlasting life." There is a choice for every sinner to make. Believe in Jesus! Jesus the Lord can be your Savior.

Let's read Romans 10:9 again. "If you confess with your mouth the Lord Jesus and believe in your heart that God has raised Him from the dead, you will be saved." Here is what you need to know:

Jesus is the Lord.
Jesus died for your sins.
God raised Him from the dead.

Jesus is alive, and He has power over everything, including death, including the things that keep you from living a life that is fulfilling.

The truth about Jesus can save you from living a life of regrets if you will believe it. You can begin to live the way God wants you to and through your actions show that you believe what you know to be true about Jesus.

When talking with friends or coworkers I'll ask them about their preferred method of communication. Usually, depending on what we are talking about, they'll respond with a text or an email. It's up to us to understand God's preferred method of communication is prayer.

Prayer is our number one way of talking to God. Through speaking, journaling, singing, and so forth, we should pray. Right now you can talk to Jesus. Ask that He become the Lord of your life and save you from your sin. Remember that sin is living the way you want to instead of the way God wants you to. It's okay if you don't know what to say. It's okay that praying feels unnatural. You are created by God, and He wants to hear from you. (A salvation prayer is provided for you in the appendix if you are looking for a guide.)

Now, let's talk about how the Bible changes us; the role of the Holy Spirit when we read our Bibles; and how that understanding helps us to live a powerful life in practical ways.

- 3 -

Power Comes from the Word

How the Bible Changes Our Lives for Real

If you do an online search for "How to change your life," the result will be a great set of lists and articles on improving the quality of your life and finding fulfillment. Have you ever wondered how you can change your life? Honestly, I didn't scroll through this search exhaustively, but the lists I read were all incomplete. Real change is initiated by only one person, and that person was not included on these lists. God is the person with the power to create change in our lives, specifically change that is healthy and includes growth—not a decaying kind of change. We do our part by surrendering to His will and doing things His way, beginning with reading the Bible and finding out who God is, who I am, how He sees me, and what my purpose is.

God's Word always initiates the formation (or transformation) of anything that turns into something new. Nothing can actually change before God is involved. Even the Bible says in the book of Ecclesiastes, "History merely repeats itself. It has all been done before. Nothing under the sun is truly new" (1:9 NLT). We are always looking for ways to improve our lives; we will always have a sense of deficit and loss on our own. The only one who can make every day meaningful is the one who created us and knows our days. Yet the road to transformation truly never ends, because we begin to recognize that we can't stay the same and we need God.

I have experienced two different situations, at the same time, where I struggled to relate to two different women. These ladies weren't friends with each other; the timing was just the same.

In January of that particular year, both situations started bothering me a lot, and I wasn't OK with the gap that was being created because of our differences. I talked with my husband about it, and he assured me I had done nothing wrong. But still the relationship gap was there, and I couldn't get it off my mind. For three months I tried calling to set up a lunch or coffee date with these individuals and would get no response.

Finally, I prayed and asked, "God, what am I not seeing? Show me my blind spot." Have you ever done that? Asked to see your weakness? Not asking about sin, but asking "what am I not good at?" "Where is my humanity?" That sounds sort of complex, I know I wasn't sure it was even the right thing to say at the time, but I decided to pray and ask anyway. It was quite a vulnerable question, actually.

Over the next few days, I read my Bible, and my mind was stuck on the story of Esther. I had the idea to look at the story from someone else's perspective. Instead of putting myself in Esther's shoes, the way most preachers suggest, I decided to put myself in the king's shoes and think about what it would be like to be the king in this story.

Have you heard this incredible story? Esther was an orphan, who was also a slave in the kingdom of Persia. Through the sovereign positioning of God, she became the queen of Persia! When the king of Persia was being deceived by an old friend, Esther was able to bring the truth to light and save an entire race from death.

It was then that I could see my blind spot! Esther is one historical account I find myself in constantly. Through reading the Bible and studying the history and background of a story, we can begin to ask what it would be like to be one of the people in that culture and time. Through this process of study and meditation, the Holy Spirit can show us things to think about and things to do differently in our lives today, based on the example of people who lived the way God wanted them to live in their day.

My Blind Spot

When I put myself in the position of the king, with supreme decision-making authority, I realized my blind spot was Haman, whose advice caused me to make the wrong choice. Both of my situations were "Esther" situations that revealed to me an area in my life I could improve on, though I was unaware at the time. You see, the king trusted and relied on Haman. He took advice from Haman. Haman may have earned the king's trust by issuing good advice in the past, but he made the mistake of attempting to use the truth against the king for his own power and influence. What I have learned is that truth used against you is twisted truth. Truth is always for you!

Twisted truth is a lie—it is manipulation—and God is not a manipulator. God brought Esther to the palace at a particular time because of His loving-kindness for the Jews; and through Esther's political position, she was able to reveal the real truth about Haman's advice to the king at a dinner she hosted. The heart of hospitality will always create a space to tell the truth in love.

So, back to my blind spot. I began to ask God "What is my Haman?" What is keeping me from seeing the whole truth? When I asked this question I began to see that the Lord wanted to develop in me a gift of mercy.

The gap between myself and these two other individuals was (for me) that I was trying to have a friendship my way. Had I done anything wrong to them? No, nothing is wrong with trying to set up coffee; however, forcing something, including friendship, on someone else is wrong.

The entire time the Holy Spirit was touching a nerve. I love people; I'm a people- pleaser by nature. I have learned, though, to trust that God's affirmation is enough. If people don't want to be my friend, my value is not diminished.

Notice that my actions weren't wrong. In fact, the steps I took are the right ones to take when making friends and building community. But there are moments when the right thing becomes the wrong thing if it's being used against you or someone else; or, in my case, against my own self. God doesn't force us into a relationship with Him, yet He remains faithful to us and has made His Word available every day to help us discern what is right and when the time is right.

How Does the Bible Change Our Lives?

We have to let the Bible change our lives, reveal blind spots, help us overcome sin, and we must stand strong in our Christian beliefs by building healthy habits. Honesty moment: This is a hard thing to do, so I'm thankful someone else is in charge. That someone else is Jesus Christ.

We let the Bible change our lives by reading it regularly. This is the most practical thing we can do. Having a Bible on your shelf, or in an app on your phone, doesn't give you the power to overcome sin or make confident, effective choices for your health, your business, or your future. When we consistently read the Bible, over time, as we submit our time, our minds, and discipline ourselves, we are submitting to the process of change in our lives. What we believe to be true will eventually show through our actions.

We must let the Bible show us how to live with Jesus as our Lord and Savior. Knowing God through His Word and knowing how He wants us to behave makes our choices powerful. As you read the Bible, two very practical things happen, and I want to develop these two ideas briefly. The Holy Spirit's choices are effective, while our choices are affected.

Because the Holy Spirit's choices are effective, He
- leads us into all truth;
- leads us into long-term freedom;
- helps us to be familiar with what God wants;
- leads us to repentance;
- gives us the power to forgive others, as we have been forgiven;
- transforms us;
- reveals the truth that empowers us;
- guides us into all truth;
- changes the way we think;
- and helps us to not be conformed to the patterns and customs of this world, but to be transformed by the renew-

ing of our minds, so we will be able to test and prove God's will —His good, pleasing, and perfect will (Romans 12:2).

Our Choices are affected in that we
- find the truth;
- rehearse the truth;
- set our mind on God's ways;
- repent;
- forgive;
- read more of the Bible (and then realize our dependence on God so then we read more);
- listen until we understand;
- learn new thought patterns, define and break bad habits, and overcome sin;
- develop new brain pathways (those little connections in our brain!), which over time can change the connections in our minds and actions;
- change the way we think;
- and learn Scripture.

Do you see how these two lists pair up? What else do you notice about your life when you read the Bible or obey God? When we let the Bible change us, we make different and better decisions because of the knowledge we have gained about God and Kingdom living.

When we have the Holy Spirit guiding us, we can be confident in our decisions. The amazing thing about reading the Bible is that it is God's Word. And just as His spoken word created the world and all of creation, God's written, inspired Word initiates change in our lives. If something about us hasn't grown, increased, or transformed, we should ask ourselves these three questions:

1. Is this thing (my character, this habit, my identity, or anything else) supposed to change?
2. What does the Bible say about this thing?
3. How often do I read my Bible and pray about this?

We cannot sit down and answer these questions in an afternoon. This is an ongoing search, a quest for something more, a reach for change that ultimately affects our entire lives and can set us up for a life of no regrets. When I speak of "no regrets," I'm not saying we are perfect. We sin and we need to repent, also have human limitations but the closer to the Lord we get, the more we can lean on the Holy Spirit and be free from shame and living our entire lives in a state of emotional distress. Holiness isn't perfection. God isn't asking us to be perfect. He is asking us to be holy.

God uses our unbelief, our problems, and our imperfections to reveal His glory. There is nothing to regret when God is involved—just a deep sense of gratitude toward Him for saving us from ourselves and our old ways.

Steps for Change

If we aren't the initiators of change, how do we join in the process of change and live the way God wants us to live? Changing our thinking takes advance planning and allowing ourselves to be different; only then we can learn to be OK with knowing what to do and being uncomfortable through the process. The first step is to give up control of how we think the change process should look and give up control of how the end result will look.

Think of it this way: When individuals vote for a local politician, they surrender their influence to the politician's name. If elected, this person becomes the representative of his or her constituents. The people give control or power to the one elected to make decisions for his or her community, and the elected official gets to effect the end result. In your daily decisions to whom are you surrendering your influence? Who has the last word in your situations?

We can trust that God is faithful to complete what He started, that He will not abandon us, and that He will give us a good future—a life with no regrets. Again, I say "no regrets," because when our bad choices are forgiven, we can learn from our past, and even bad choices become valuable. God is sovereign and can take everything that is out of order and create order from it (Genesis 50:20). When we recognize how far we are from God's plans and purpose, the process of God working out all things the devil meant for evil begins. God can use even our worst moments to help us live powerful lives.

Giving up control also means we don't need to worry or be anxious. Worry is the opposite of trust. Worry breaks down faith. Worry is rooted in fear. Worry says, "What if this time something good doesn't happen?" "What if what God said isn't true?" This is the same question Eve considered in the garden. It's the same thought that deceived the first couple who walked the earth—a fear that God won't be to me what the Bible promises! If every promise in the book is mine, then I must trust that God is able to do exceedingly, abundantly more than I think He can (Ephesians 3:20). And, in order to claim those promises, we must know them!

Have you read about King David? Have you ever thought about what made him such a great king? It wasn't because he was perfect. Oh, man; did he ever make some horrible, selfish choices! But he knew God because he understood God's ways. David found his connection with God through Scripture, which, at that time, was the Pentateuch (Genesis through Deuteronomy; aka, the Law of Moses). David rehearsed the Word of God regularly, and he wrote some of the psalms. Note King David's words in Psalm 63:

So I will bless You as long as I live;
I will lift up my hands in Your name . . . .
When I remember You on my bed,
I meditate and thoughtfully focus on You
in the night watches. (verses 4, 6 AMP)

In a later chapter we will discuss more about David and the different seasons of obeying God; but, for now, let us continue through the process of change.

The second step to experiencing change is rehearsing the stories or inspiring verses that you read from the Bible, the way David did. As we pray and rehearse (or meditate) on the Word, our perspective changes. For example, when I decided to think about the story of Esther from a different angle. The Holy Spirit will lead us into all truth (John 16:13) as we position our minds to learn and know the truth. As our perspective is changed, we must plan to act differently, which is step three. This is not an exhaustive list, but here are some things you can do to facilitate change in your life:

- Talk to your friends and family about what you are learning.
- Create a budget and stick to it.
- Change the way you treat people.
- Change your schedule to avoid locations and people who influence you negatively.
- Change your schedule to reflect a more Kingdom-focused life (serving, giving, spending time with other Christians).
- Pray more.
- Attend church weekly.
- Serve at your church regularly (don't flake out).
- Stop doing drugs (ask for help).
- Stop hurting people around you or being around people who hurt you.
- Stop having casual sex, don't use pornography or perform other unhealthy sexual actions.
- Avoid overeating, emotional eating, or not eating at all.
- Focus on caring more about people than on being right.
- Focus more on sharing the truth than worrying about being accepted.
- Find a mentor.

What one thing can you change in your life that would show Jesus is your Lord?

Finally, step four. Stay committed to the process of change and don't stop. Even if it's difficult, even if you mess up, and when life gets busy. If we change our actions because of what we read in the Bible, we have allowed the power of God's Word to change our lives. And it doesn't stop there! As we continue we will begin to recognize the power of the Word in our lives and how fulfilling it is to obey God. Then, when we mess up, we recognize our dependency on Jesus Christ, and His grace keeps us going. This is called living a Spirit-led life.

When we let the Holy Spirit lead us in our decisions, we can find a sense of achievement and can be confident we are doing the right thing. At times, though, we may feel loss, because there is always a cost to following Jesus. When we change, we can sometimes feel as if we are losing control of our lives and surrendering them to someone else. This includes situations like when or how we choose to respond to criticism on social media, and how we respond to someone else's mistake.

If we are following the Holy Spirit our actions will result in things like self-control, patience, and faithfulness. If we are leading ourselves or following another human's agenda it's easy to justify ourselves, to feel like we have to defend ourselves, and prove ourselves. Learning to rely on the Holy Spirit and let the Lord be our defense is one of the hardest lessons I have had to learn in life, but it's rewarding. I can see clearly and make decisions more confidently. And so can you!

Think about the words in this verse: "Don't copy the behavior and customs [ways] of this world, but let God transform you into a new person by changing the way you think. Then you will learn to know God's will for you, which is good and pleasing and perfect" (Romans 12:2 NLT).

When we draw closer to God, we learn more about how our relationship with Him should work. This is what the second half of Romans 12:2 means: "Then you will learn to know God's will for you, which is good and pleasing and perfect." What has changed in your life since you became a Christian?

Psalm 63

O God, You are my God;
Early will I seek You;
My soul thirsts for You;
My flesh longs for You
In a dry and thirsty land
Where there is no water.
So I have looked for You in the sanctuary,
To see Your power and Your glory.

Because Your lovingkindness is better than life,
My lips shall praise You.
Thus I will bless You while I live;
I will lift up my hands in Your name.
My soul shall be satisfied as with marrow and fatness,
And my mouth shall praise You with joyful lips.
When I remember You on my bed,
I meditate on You in the night watches.
Because You have been my help,
Therefore in the shadow of Your wings I will rejoice.
My soul follows close behind You;
Your right hand upholds me.

But those who seek my life, to destroy it,
Shall go into the lower parts of the earth.
They shall fall by the sword;
They shall be a portion for jackals.

But the king shall rejoice in God;
Everyone who swears by Him shall glory;

But the mouth of those who speak lies shall be stopped.

Psalm 63 was my favorite chapter as a young adult. What do you think King David meant when he said that he was satisfied?

The apostle Paul said, "Since, then, you have been raised with Christ, set your hearts on things above, where Christ is, seated at the right hand of God. Set your mind on things above, not on earthly things" (Colossians 3:1-2 NIV). What are some things you should stop thinking about? What are some things you should start to think about?

When we read the Bible, we gain knowledge. We learn about God, His Spirit (the Holy Spirit), and we learn a lot about Jesus in the New Testament. When we study how the three persons of the trinity act, and how they engage with creation and humans specifically, we can understand better what is expected of us. Then, based on what we understand, we can decide to behave in a certain way. This is called wisdom. People who know the Bible but don't live according to its principles are foolish (Luke 6:46-49).

We gain wisdom first through acquiring knowledge and then by understanding it. Worldly pleasures will satisfy for a season, but we will find ourselves living unfulfilled and ineffective again (Romans 12:2). When we truly change our minds about changing our lifestyle, there is always grace from Jesus as our Lord and Savior. He died so that change would be our reality. "My grace is sufficient for you, for my power is made perfect in weakness." Therefore I will boast all the more gladly about my weaknesses, so that Christ's power may rest on me" (2 Corinthians 12:9 NIV).

The Lord told Paul, "My grace is sufficient for you." The same is true for us today. God's grace is sufficient when we rehearse the Bible in our thoughts and keep our minds on His ways, regardless of what other facts tell us. And I do believe we should know all the facts! Still, when Christ's power rests on us, our lives will change. Amen!

- 4 -

Power Comes from His Words

During my early twenties, I was part of a church-plant team, worked full-time in a retail store at the mall, and attended Boise State University for two semesters. I made more money during that time period than I have since. I bought clothes all the time and had six coffees almost daily. I hung out with friends and served my church with all my heart. Yet, even with all of that, I knew something wasn't right inside of me. I was going a hundred miles an hour in the wrong direction. I was a little bit off-track, but a little bit off is all the way off! A little bit wrong is all wrong. A little sin makes us completely sinful.

I wasn't making bad choices, according to my own logic, but I also wasn't considering the greatness of God and basing my choices off of that. I was working so hard, yet finding limited fulfillment, even though I was checking off the right boxes. I was just living—believing for something big to happen for me—and doing what was expected of me because that's what people do at this age. I was just letting life happen to me as it came; and even though I wanted more out of life, I was exhausted. Eventually I started losing friends, hating church, and not liking who I was (apart from the church); I didn't know what I wanted to do with my life. Making friends after losing friends is hard. Add to that the fact that I'm a high-functioning introvert. I wasn't healthy, and I couldn't fix myself.

I have to say that keeping myself busy serving at church and reading the Bible has preserved me during the seasons when I felt as if I was swimming upstream and in moments I hurt the most. I have always known God is near and has plans for my life. But it sometimes felt as if I was far from those plans and not good enough to achieve them. I was just a good church kid. But being good and being a church kid isn't enough.

I was living to contribute MY story to HIStory
instead of simply living in response to HIS greatness.

I remember one particular conversation with my mom during that time that concluded with the decision that I should apply to Bible college. The college I was looking at was out of state; and though the school was somewhat familiar to our family, I'd be alone, have to find a new job, and go to a new church. I would be starting over, and I had just ended a season of starting over! I remember being exhausted and burned out. But this time my focus had shifted.

So I moved to Portland, Oregon, a city I had visited as a child during Christmas, so I was fairly familiar with it; but I got lost probably half a dozen times. It was frustrating. I was late to at least three job interviews. I'm nice, but quiet, until you really get to know me, and I don't open up easily. Then school started. Now this I could do—sit in class, take notes, and learn about the Bible. I loved the Bible then, and still do. But I didn't realize the deep (spiritual) heart surgery that would begin to take place inside of me. I would sit in the back and cry through every class. God had begun a work in me, which I'll bet He was excited about it, but I was drained and broken into pieces. I was worn-out; my spiritual heartbeat was off rhythm, though still beating. Everything in my life had changed so fast, like a car on the freeway when the side view is blurry. I had only one thing to stand on and believe in. Not church, not money, not family or friends. The Word of God.

One day my fireball roommate asked, "Are you OK?" I told her I had just finished the hardest season I have ever been through in my life. During the next few weeks I went to class saying to myself, "This stuff is real" (meaning the theology I was learning) and "I'm going to believe it is all real for me." I remember clearly walking into the classroom building one foggy, cold morning telling myself this and choosing to believe the Word of God was true for me.

Now, even though I was receiving four hours of biblical education Monday through Friday, not everything was easy or even showing progress. The information I was being taught was only a seed being planted in the soil of my life. I had to choose every day to believe it was real and it could change my life, over time. I had to accept that power in the practical steps comes from the Word of God. I had to keep thinking about it all day in order to surrender to it in all areas. But, thankfully, I wasn't alone. Jesus believed that power was in the Word too!

Jesus believed the Word.

39

Satan has power. Did you know that? It's limited, but he, too, has influence on the earth and in our lives if we let him have it. Did you know he tried to use his influence to manipulate Jesus? Can you believe it? Let me summarize this historical moment for you.

In Matthew 4, we see Jesus in the wilderness. He was led there by the Holy Spirit and was there for forty days. In Matthew's account, Jesus was praying and fasting to receive from God direction and power to make the right choices in the days to come. He needed power to do miracles, teach the Word, and, ultimately, accomplish God's will for His life, which was to die for our sins and be the Savior of the world (John 3:16).

During that time Satan tried to tempt Jesus. Satan tried to get Jesus to give him power (influence) by tempting Jesus to worship him or acknowledge Satan's position of influence. But Jesus told him, "No! The Scriptures say, 'People do not live by bread alone, but by every word that comes from the mouth of God.'" (Deuteronomy 8:3 NLT) Jesus believed the Word, and used it as His source of power when tempted.

Unpacking the Story

Remember, prayer is our number one way of talking to God. Prayer is sometimes accompanied with fasting. Fasting is a process of eliminating something from our lives in order to focus our minds and remove things that would distract us from receiving what God has for us during the conversation. Usually people fast from food; but for health reasons, or if the whole family participates, you can give up other things such as secular music, social media, or sugar. Fasting enhances the clarity of our senses as God speaks to us, even though we are really, really hungry. Hunger is not a sense but an appetite—an appetite created by God to remind us we need energy. Food is our bodies' source of power. However, when we fast, we are taking time out of our schedule, budgets, hobbies and projects, to show God that we believe our true source of power (ability) is found in Him. We are also scheduling time to focus on Him for guidance, healing, breakthrough, or the effectiveness to accomplish something in our lives.

So, let's go back to the story of Satan offering power to Jesus. I want to be specific about something here: Satan didn't lie to Jesus. He tried to deceive Jesus by twisting the truth. Remember how Haman twisted the truth in Esther's experience? I have found clarity in confusing situations when I remember that twisted truth is also truth diluted. One of Satan's tools is to twist the truth, which weakens our ability to live God's way. We might be making spiritually thoughtful decisions; but if they don't contain the whole truth, they won't help us.

Usually, when I can identify the twisted truth that I have believed, I also find a lie that has limited me and caused me to live in a way that is contrary to how God created me to live. For me, it's usually acting in fear and shying away from saying something or doing something.

When we read Matthew 4:4, we see that Satan reminded Jesus of His ability to do miracles, which is true. He also taunted Jesus, reminding Him of His need, food, for which we have a real (God-created) appetite. Satan tried to deceive Jesus by distracting Him with the truth (about Jesus the man) that could satisfy a real need. Jesus responded with another truth that satisfies more than a physical need and settles the power dispute. He said no. His response shows us that even the Son of God used the Word of God to live a powerful life.

Taking My Cue from Jesus

Here are two thoughts about Jesus being tempted and untwisting the twisted truth. First, Jesus responded to the power struggle with Scripture. If I am supposed to get through this blurry life, I, too, have to quote Scripture. And to quote Scripture, I have to know it first, by reading or hearing it. Second, Jesus responded to Satan's twisted truth about Jesus' abilities with the real truth about God's abilities. When I face temptation, it's not my abilities I should trust in—it's God's abilities. Second Corinthians 12:9 tells us that God's grace is sufficient and Christ's power will rest on us in these times!

Five verses from the Bible talk about the power of the Word of God. These were the verses that began my journey in trusting that I can be powerful and practical, "un-twisting" the twisted truth. Consider beginning your powerful living by doing something practical. Memorize these verses and trust that they are true:

In the beginning was the Word, and the Word was with God, and the Word was God. He was in the beginning with God. (John 1:1-2)

For I am not ashamed of the gospel of Jesus Christ, for it is the power of God to salvation for everyone who believes, for the Jew first and also for the Greek. For in it the righteousness of God is revealed from faith to faith; as it is written, "The just shall live by faith." (Romans 1:16-17)

So then faith comes by hearing, and hearing by the word of God. (Romans 10:17)

All Scripture is given by inspiration of God, and is profitable for doctrine, for reproof, for correction, for instruction in righteousness, that the man of God may be complete, thoroughly equipped for every good work. (2 Timothy 3:16-17)

For the Word of God is living and powerful, and sharper than any two-edged sword, piercing even to the division of the soul and spirit, and of joints and marrow, and is a discerner of the thoughts and intents of the heart. (Hebrews 4:12)

Satan's Strategy

The Holy Spirit is always leading us to seek after and surrender to God. We should be aware of and prepare for what Satan did to Jesus by being familiar with Scripture.

When we know the real truth, the twisted truth won't sit right in our hearts and minds; something won't make sense. As we search for truth by reading the Bible, the Holy Spirit is faithful to reveal it to us. This will keep us from giving into temptation and sinning!

John 16:13 in the New Living Translation says "When the Spirit of truth comes, he will guide you into all truth. He will not speak on his own but will tell you what he has heard." We can't get impatient in our search. We must search for the truth until we know it, and the way Jesus responded to Satan is how we also should respond—with Scripture. We can do as Jesus did but only by being familiar with Scripture first.

The effects of deception (twisted truth) and distraction (diluted truth) are sin. Sin in the original Greek is defined as "missing the mark" or "failure."[1] Think of an archer who releases his arrow, only to find he misses his target. He has failed to accomplish what he set out to do. He was deceived; possibly his depth perception was off or he was distracted. Proverbs 29:18 in The Amplified Bible says, "Where there is no vision [no revelation of God and His word], the people are unrestrained; But happy and blessed is he who keeps the law [of God]." We have a choice to look at our own abilities and try to satisfy our needs instead of looking at Christ and following His ways for fulfillment.

Satan wants to render us powerless by deceiving or distracting us. Or both! Actually, always both. We cannot let him have the power in our lives! And many Christians do so by not surrendering to Jesus Christ as their Lord, even when they have accepted Him as their Savior.

Satan desires us to be like him. He was once in right relationship with God, worshiping God and giving Him glory. However Satan was distracted, and then deceived, which ultimately ended with a great (and permanent) separation between him and the God of the universe.

Satan's strategy is to deceive us into thinking we will be fulfilled if we satisfy a temporary and real need by using our God-given abilities. He will distract us with things that are a part of us, but are not a part of our identity, which can only come from our Creator. Satan's goal is to draw us away from a Kingdom mind-set; he wants us to think about and trust in our abilities, instead of God's abilities, and to do things his way. The only way Satan can give us power is if we first give it to him by fueling the distraction and deception with emotions and thoughts that are focused on ourselves or our problems instead of Jesus Christ. We possess the power of free will. In other words, God gave us the power to choose.

Can I ask you, is there a real need in your life that is distracting? Do you rehearse in your mind or have conversations that give you permission to avoid growth and change? How are these "twisted truth"?

Any "truth" that encourages us to sin is deception. When we are familiar with Scripture, we have the opportunity and ability to compare when God is trying to lead us and when Satan is trying to deceive us. You are smart enough to discern between the two, and God can make you wise enough. You just have to know His Word! You have to read the book and hear from God. Satan will use the truth against us, and it's important to know the Bible so we can stay under the power (influence) of the Lord and not Satan. This will help us hear God in difficult times and bring clarity to our minds.

How to Hear God

Now you might be asking, "How can I hear God?" It's an important question. This blog post I wrote in 2018 answers the question.

I believe God is real and clearly communicates His heart and intentions towards people. Practically speaking though, hearing God isn't easy. These days you can text a counselor and you'll hear back within 24 hours, but it doesn't seem like it's that easy to hear from God, and God is everywhere. Always there . . . but not always heard.

We can get so distracted by good things, being passionate about a cause, starting a family and pursuing a career. Wrong things done to us & wrong things we have done can also affect how we hear God. To make it more complicated, those of us who hear God, would say we "hear" differently. Some people hear God through visions, feelings, ideas, circumstances, nature, the list goes on . . . and even though we all hear God differently, we all are called (and expected by God) to live by the same standard. That standard is the Bible. No other message from any method of "hearing" is greater than the message we read from the Bible. (Read that sentence again, it's true!) The Bible is the standard. If what God is communicating to us, doesn't line up with the Bible, then I question if it's God speaking. It could be just a really big, good idea. It could also be an easy way out of addressing a situation we should address.

Three things I know about hearing God:

1. The Bible is Gods number one way of talking to us.
2. Hearing God takes discipline; it is a process you must practice.
3. If we aren't reading our Bible, we can't hear clearly.

When I read the Bible I don't hear an audible voice like I just pressed play on a podcast. I read the Bible in my own voice, but I read to hear God. How? When I read, I look for His words and actions. I become aware of how He leads individuals or people groups. When they obey or don't obey, I look for Gods response to it. If God is the same, yesterday, today and forever, (Hebrews 13:8) then I can trust that when I obey or disobey, God will lead me the same way. This is what I look for. I look for "Gods ways." That is how to hear God, by reading and studying, looking for Him through the pages of the written Word.

So in order to hear God daily, I need to be reading the Bible daily. Daily learning how He thinks and what His intentions are for me. I need to let those ideas impact my attitudes and choices.

46

I believe God will support His word with The Word. I believe He will speak to you if you will listen, and read your Bible. Hearing = Reading.[2]

Let me connect the dots now: Hearing God, then obeying what He says, can help us overcome temptation, sin, and help us live a spirit-led life.

If Jesus, in the middle of an earthly need, relied on Scripture as His source of power to live and avoid deception, then my conviction is that I need to rely on the scriptures for effective living as well. And if Jesus, the Son of Man, overcame, then so can you and I.

Consider the following

In Jeremiah 33:3 God said, "Call to Me, and I will answer you, and show you great and mighty things, which you do not know." Is there something in your life right now that seems too impossible to face? The psalmist once wrote in Psalm 119:105, "Your word is a lamp to my feet, and a light to my path."

Jesus was hungry. It was a condition he experienced at that time but it was not a sin. We, too, get hungry in our lives. We have a desire for something more. It is a state that causes us to surrender to something stronger than we are. Jesus (the Son of man) needed power to accomplish God's will for His life, which was to save all of humanity. What area in your life is weak? Remember Colossians 3:1-2? Daily we must fill our minds with what the Bible says about the weak areas of our lives. One practical question you might ask is: How do I get the Word of God inside of me if I can't go to church every day to hear preaching? Here are some ways to put the Bible in your mind:

- Put an appointment in your calendar to pray, then keep the appointment. You are meeting with God.
- Podcasts
- Apps
- Music with Christian lyrics
- Phone screen (locked and home screens)
- Sticky notes on the bathroom mirror, in your locker, or on your desktop
- Worship music
- Church blogs
- Follow accounts on social media that post Bible verses
- Cut three-by-five cards in half and write verses on them that you intend to memorize. Hole punch them and put them all on a key ring. Then, instead of looking at social media when you are waiting in lines or during down time, look through those Bible verses. Keep them in your pocket.
- Bible studies with other people
- Paint Bible verses
- Make up songs using Bible verses as the lyrics
- Post an image of a Bible verse to social media so that when you look at your profile, you see it.
- Add posters, images, or sticky notes to your wall in the kitchen, on your fridge or inside your cupboards.
- Get rid of things that don't have biblically inspired content.
- Just read it; consider audio if your hands are full. Reading one chapter a day is a good start. Read Proverbs for wisdom, Psalms for a brief history of the Bible and to worship God, and the book of John to get to know Jesus.

Remember, it's not a competition. Read the Bible slow enough to see and remember how God treats His people. Notice what words He uses to describe His feelings about them. Read it for yourself. Read it to know how much God loves you, and how much your life can be impacted.

- 5 -

Power Comes from Understanding Times and Seasons

One night, when I was seventeen years old, I was sitting at the bar in our kitchen gluing dried rose petals to a piece of parchment paper. I was working on a piece of art I planned to frame. While I was sitting there, my parents said goodbye and left for a vacation to Jamaica. Now my family is a normal family, so when I tell my younger siblings to do something, they don't listen. So, even though I was old enough to be home alone for a week, my little brother still needed someone to help him get to basketball practice and see that he did his homework and completed his chores while our parents were gone. That someone couldn't be me.

Later that same night, a good-looking nineteen-year-old guy, who was my brother's designated chauffeur, walked into our house, while I was still gluing crumbly, red roses onto the paper. I said hi and then mostly ignored him the rest of the night, because I'm awesome and awkward like that. I remember so clearly knowing this was the guy I was going to marry. But I also knew saying something at that moment would be totally creepy, so I didn't.

Almost seven years later, I did marry that guy. I married my first boyfriend, my first kiss, Mr. Trevin Anderson. Now the journey to marriage wasn't easy. In fact, we had the opportunity to get it wrong, really wrong. We were told we couldn't date. We could have been impatient; we could have said we were adults and could do what we wanted. We could have spent too much time alone together and said, "Everyone has sex before marriage nowadays." We really could have. Yes, waiting for God's timing increases the pressure to be impatient, give up, or give into temptation; but the power of our choices increases when we make the right ones. Let's look at the idea of timing and seasons.

Ready! Get Set! Go!

Every season of life has a "Ready! Get Set! Go!" pattern. For example, when my husband and I got married, our marriage was in the Go! season—so was having sex! Before that, we were in a season of getting ready for marriage and stewarding our sexuality, dreaming, and maturing to someday be someone's spouse. During our married Go! season we entered a Ready! season, as we dreamed and discussed the idea of having children. Then we began to Get Set! as a team, setting in place expectations, finances, and working on our communication skills. In one particular area of our lives we might be ready, while in other areas of our lives we are still getting set into position, or we are already living the dream and going.

In order to Go! and do what we believe God is inviting and asking us to do, we must submit to and embrace the Ready! and Get set! times that are required first. If you ignore or resist Ready! and Get set!, you delay the Go!. If you try to take a shortcut, you could delay the Go! or end up living a different Go! So, take the right steps of faith, be led by the Holy Spirit by reading your Bible on a daily basis, and submit to God's timing.

Understanding Seasons

When we look at time, we can see patterns in our lives. In Genesis 1:14, God created time and seasons. Sometimes, seasons overlap and knowing how to prepare and respond during those seasons can become complicated. I'm hoping to unpack the idea of timing and seasons to help you see how you can make right choices and increase your chances of living an effective and influential life.

When making choices it's important to know what season you are in and where you are going. Timing should have some effect on your choices. For example, in a year (on the calendar) we can see a pattern of seasons: winter, spring, summer, and fall. My family lives in the great Pacific Northwest. It rains a lot here, and winters have a biting wind that stings my skin and only a little snow to make the holidays magical and almost worth the chill. Our spring and fall are very wet and usually gray; but on the flip side, our summers are hot, and we love them.

When we plan vacations to a beach location, we will leave the cold of spring or gray of fall to enjoy the weather in some other sunny place. Our timing is important! We honestly love the Northwest during the summer. It's like living in a vacation spot on your day off and sometimes on your lunch break. The Pacific Northwest is stunning—very relaxing—and there are so many amazing things to do here for people of all ages. So we plan around the summer and go somewhere sunny during the cold months when we need a break from the gray.

Likewise, the approaching of fall is my signal or reminder that winter is coming, and I go to our garage and unpack the boxes with our snow pants, gloves, boots, and scarves so that I can have our kids try them on to see if these items still fit. If they don't fit we save up some money, wait for some good on-line deals, or we look through hand-me downs from an older cousin. We plan ahead so that we are prepared for life and can continue to enjoy it regardless of the season. We can do the same in all areas of life, not just with the weather or our closets.

The idea is the same with the Lord and living a Spirit-led life. We can see and know patterns in our lives; and as we notice these, we can prepare for them and know contentment even in the middle of some of the worst situations. Let me be real here: life is hard—it's lonely, it's gut-wrenchingly painful—and that fact escapes no one.

Shortly after Trevin and I moved to Oregon, he was injured during a turkey bowl game. He had the ball, and a big dude tackled him (it was supposed to be two-touch, not tackle!). But what happened next was a moment that affected the next three years of our finances. His knee inverted. I remember getting the call from our friend who was driving him to the emergency room. Trevin couldn't work and was put on short-term disability through the holidays. Our funds were so tight we bought our son three toys from the Target dollar section and the dollar store.

To add to the misery, it was just us, we were alone, with no invitations to holiday parties and the weather was cold. Then, six months later, our two-year-old broke his arm. Later that year our renters left our rental house without notice, and we were swamped with bills, no help, and no hope for a raise. This drained our savings so fast. Thank God for the savings; but when it was dried up, it was stressful! Trevin went through a season of depression. He experienced anxiety attacks, and I think for the first time he started truly grieving the loss of his mother.[1] I had no clue how to handle any of this. I had only the Bible and a few counseling courses from college that I could refer to.

In the middle of all this, I was doing the Beth Moore Bible study on Esther[2] and praying. I told God, "This is not how we are called to live. We will overcome this." I wrote two goals on a sticky note and put that sticky note on one of my cupboard doors in the kitchen. Those two goals were: (1) Keep the house clean; and (2) Feed the boys well. I told God I was committing to nothing but these two things and stewarding well what He had given me.

During this low time in our health and finances we were in a spiritual battle to believe there was more for us. I honestly believe that because of our faith in Christ, our faithfulness to each other, and our stewardship of our health and finances, we saw a brighter day.

Did we ask for this difficult season? No. Were we ready? Is anyone ever really ready for rough seasons? I believe we can be somewhat ready. When life is going well that is the time to prepare for accidents and rough situations by staying teachable, reading books, meeting with pastors, reminding ourselves of God's promises, and working hard to have a savings. And it is the same with seasons of enjoyment and success. I find that if I'm not prepared for the good moments, then I don't remember them or enjoy them as much. I let the goals I am trying to reach or the busyness of life get in my way. I get into performance mode instead of just being present. Being organized and staying honest help me stay present. I forget to celebrate if I'm not ready. Preparing for the cold seasons during the warm seasons of our lives is practical and powerful living.

Preparation in the different times and seasons of life is practical and powerful. We can even prepare for seasons in a spiritually way. We can be Spirit-led through the best and the worst seasons of our lives, but the choice is a focused one. Sometimes we have to grit our teeth and press on. When we stop and notice different moments in our lives, we can see the Ready! Get Set! Go! pattern. We can look at the seasons of our lives, know where we have come from, and dream about what is to come. There is power in the practical steps of walking through each season and letting the timing be in God's hands.

I have found that God will give us a word or a desire; specifically, a cause for which to fight, a habit to break, or a dream to chase, such as going to college, getting married, being healthy, having children, living debt-free, or finishing a project. Each of these can happen for us in time, and we can look back and be proud of our choices. Of course we can't make these things happen overnight. Instant success isn't real but a filter on life that others have bought into. And, if someone does have instant success, it's because of someone else's hard work and sacrifice; it's never just instant. You can't microwave lasting success; it's a "slow cooker" experience. You know it's coming, and you just have to be patient.

Every healthy desire or goal to be a functioning adult who contributes to his or her community has a Ready! Get Set! Go! pattern. Also every word from God has a Ready! Get Set! Go! pattern.

Let's look at each stage in the pattern briefly while looking at the life of David the king of Israel in the Old Testament. Then we'll bring it around to living powerfully in the practical situations of our own lives. When we understand the pattern we can identify where we are in the different layers of our lives and have the power to make the best choices, because we will see ourselves on a journey, in a season, instead of in the moment. Living in the moment can cripple our ability to know the times and seasons, and our ability to make the most of them is hampered. Let's look at the Ready! season.

Ready!

God will point us out, so that we receive His invitation to surrender and serve Him, and so that we realize how important we are to Him, because He loves us—you—so much! Some people will say "God has called you" or "you are called." Basically that means they, or you, notice that God has dreams and assignments for you that He wants you to start dreaming about and pursuing.

In 1 Samuel 16, we see that David's Ready! Get set! Go! pattern for kingship begins. We read in verse 13 that the prophet Samuel poured oil over David's head, and not a little splash, but a full horn of oil was poured over David to anoint him. The word anoint means "to choose."[3] David was chosen by God to become the king of Israel (verses 1-3). The awkward thing about this anointed moment was that Israel already had a king, Saul, and David was not his son! King Saul didn't even know David. David was a shepherd boy, the youngest of his family, who was forgotten when the prophet Samuel first arrived at their house. What a crazy idea that God chose an unknown, forgotten shepherd boy to be a king.

As I read through David's story I found some of his experiences that we, too, might have when we are in the Ready! season of a dream or a goal we would like to achieve. (Scripture references are provided for each of these and are listed in the Appendix.) These experiences are:

- God will call you.
- God will point you out to yourself so that you notice how important and valuable you are.
- Your heart motives will begin to be exposed.
- You will be tempted to become distracted by things that may seem necessary to the natural mind but may not match a Kingdom mind-set.
- You will be discouraged to not even try and just give up.
- God will show you what abilities and victories you already have.
- The goal, the calling, will seem impossible.
- You might feel a "righteous anger" at the challenges or hurdles you face. (Righteous anger is that anger that comes from understanding God's ways and knowing the challenges that oppose the truth.)
- Your focus should be on the goal and staying humble with your technique.
- You might see no change in your day-to-day responsibilities except that you now notice that God has His eye on you for something special.

- You must remember the Lord in times of pressure and opposition.
- You will need to develop a trust that God will position you in the right time to Get Set!

Now that you have looked through this list, is there a particular area of your life that is in the Ready! season? Maybe a process or experience you are barely just beginning?

Get Set!

God will position you to Get Set! and guide you into a season where you are educated and can learn to pace your schedule and the rhythm of living according to the Spirit as you walk and talk with Him. Everyday decisions will begin to be affected in this stage; and for the health of your Go! season, it's important to see that growth equals health, and pain doesn't always equal dysfunction. Sometimes pain means there is a breaking inside of us, and God, in His sovereignty, can use that pain to draw us closer to Him and make our Go! season more effective.

The Bible tells about men and women who were "called" and "anointed" to live Spirit-led lives. We can't live Spirit-led lives without the Holy Spirit, just like we can't have a kingdom mind-set without first having a king. Another aspect of the word anointed is found in the Greek meaning "empowered for a specific task."[4] When someone has the Holy Spirit in his life, he is anointed. When Samuel anointed David, he poured oil over his head, and David was empowered but not yet appointed as king. Think of anointing this way: before there is oil, an olive has to be crushed. In our lives, specifically, the difficult moments and seasons of our lives, the anointing is drawn out of us by the Holy Spirit preparing us to Go!

Years passed after David's anointing before he actually became king of Judah; then seven years later he became king of all of Israel (2 Samuel 2:4; 5:4-5). In many areas of our lives, as long as we stay faithful through the pressure, we will be able to look and see that though it took a while we were powerful in life's practical areas. The hard part is balancing all the areas for a long time. Faithfulness is a difficult characteristic to develop because it takes time. I think this is why we hear people say, "I hate having to be perfect all the time."

When I am in a new season, to help balance the layers, I prefer to focus on that one thing that is in the Ready! stage before I take on something else in the same stage. For example, starting college, planning a wedding, and starting a business all at the same time could create unnecessary pressure. Planning these Ready! moments for different times on my calendar increases my chances of being a successful student, spouse, and entrepreneur.

Progressing from the Ready! season to the Get Set! season, let's turn our focus again to David's journey. Here we find some of his experiences that we, too, might face in the Get Set! season of seeing a dream become reality.

- Education & training become valuable here.
- Opposition and misunderstandings begin to take place.
- You begin to recognize the tools and abilities God revealed and developed in you during the Ready! stage.
- (Though there will be resistance) opposition will not be able to stand against you.
- You will find true friendships.

- You'll be persecuted.
- People may have issues with you for no reason other than you are advancing in life.
- When people begin to see your growth, some will not like it.
- Allow others to share their perspective. (Wrestle with the facts, ask for prayer, get advice, do some research).
- Your moments of waiting may look like absence or be misunderstood by others.
- The goal may look further away than before.
- You will see and feel what habits and relationships must change or go away. (The Bible defines this as "counting the cost" in Luke 14:25.) All of your responsibilities will be affected.
- You may have more questions and fewer answers than you did before.
- You will have small reminders of past victories that should challenge and encourage you to stay faithful and keep your integrity in difficult times.
- It might look like nothing, but the Lord will add to you. Do not despise the small beginnings!
- It's possible to get stuck. Stay focused and keep moving forward.
- Fear, doubt, and mistakes will chase you, you will have to take courage again and again.
- Other people's lives will look more comfortable or as if they have already achieved their God idea.
- You will have opportunities to advance the wrong way. Use self-control.
- You will experience loss.

- God will bring you wisdom to help you continue to use self-control.
- Everything will be taken from you and your entire life will feel the weight of the cost, the exchange in the sacrifice. Remember: David strengthened himself in the Lord when things were painful!
- You will have to fight for what is yours! Advancement is a battle with great resistance.
- You will have opportunity to be stingy with what is yours, be generous.
- Obstacles will begin to move.
- It is healthy to grieve when your enemies and friends fall.
- Earthly authority figures and mentors may change.
- You will be challenged to despise the small beginnings, the little successes; you'll want to give up out of frustration and despise your youth. Be encouraged! Your goal and your invitation from the Lord to accomplish this desire are not lost!

As you can see, the Get Set! stage is more of a season of experiences that may have no pattern or formula; however, if we know that we are in a Get Set! Stage we can get the most out of it. Experiences become the tools we use or the story we tell to be effective in the next season and to be influential in other people's lives around us. Therefore, no season can be rushed or missed, paid for, or viewed through a filter for your benefit.

Awareness is half the battle.

Understanding where we are is important. This season develops character in us. We see the fruit of the Spirit become a reality in our lives. Through the Holy Spirit these experiences become tools that help us live according to Kingdom culture—help us to live the way God wants us to. Practical moments become powerful ones when we are aware of what they produce. These experiences create the platform to stand on in the Go! season. Everything that happens in the Get Ready! stage is necessary for the Go! stage in our lives to be successful.

Are you in the Get Set! season in a particular area of your life? Are you being prepared for something?

Go!

The Go! seasons of our lives are very exciting, but they still require faith and stewardship in our choices. Isaiah 26:3 says "You [God] will keep him [us] in perfect peace, whose mind is stayed on You, because he [we] trusts in You."

Trusting that God has prepared us and will let us know when to "Go!" is important. We can trust the Lord will lead us into seasons of transition, transformation, and, ultimately, thriving. This is living powerfully in the practical areas of our lives. Here are some examples of Go! seasons that we might face as adults:

- Moving out of our parent's house
- Going to college
- Voting
- Having a dream career (or a specific job after training)
- Being married
- Having healthy sex
- Living debt-free
- Owning a car or a house

- Raising children
- Sending grown children off to accomplish their dreams
- Trying something new
- Considering retirement
- Supporting social causes and investing in the next generation

We may recognize a few things from David's story that are a part of our Go! season. If you haven't really lived a Go! season, here are a few things to expect:

- We will see God's promises fulfilled.
- We will continue to be misunderstood and judged.
- We will need to speak our identity, address any challenges, and ignore labels.
- We will be blessed.
- We will be tempted to take it easy in moments of advancement.
- We will mess up. Let's own our mistakes and get back on track!
- Others will be effected by our decisions; team, family, opposition, etc.
- We will have victory and complete the assignment God has chosen us for and called us to.
- The Lord will be glorified through our life.
- Continually thank the Lord for everything happening in our lives.

Ready! Get Set! Go!

Stewarding and experiencing the "Ready! Get Set! Go!" seasons of life in God's timing is powerful living. For single adults, choosing to focus on your lifestyle, including what activities you engage in, how healthy you eat, serving at church, how you handle your finances, and stewarding well your sexuality before (not just inside of) marriage are all different areas where you can learn self-control and grow your capacity. In these seasons you will learn to trust yourself and what you can accomplish on your own. Trust me, these things can be accomplished with encouragement from friends and guidance from parents, pastors, mentors, and counselors if you need to unpack dysfunction from the past to truly live free.

Now, remember how I said the hard part is trying to balance all the different seasons of life? Have you ever felt the pressure to be perfect once you have reached a goal? Did you give up and then mess up? There is hope for us to live powerful, Spirit-led lives in practical ways, even after we make a decision in error. King David knew that very well. When he was king, he had an affair and had the woman's husband taken to the front of a heated battle so that he would die. King David was a homewrecker and a murderer, yet he is known throughout history as one of the greatest kings who ever lived, and God called him a man after His own heart (1 Samuel 13:14; Acts 13:22).

Though our pasts might be painful and shameful, we can live powerful lives in the present. The act of surrendering your life to Jesus your Lord and Savior includes receiving forgiveness. Yes, you may have to face consequences of your actions, as David did, but restoration is still available to you. Let's talk about being imperfect and still living a Spirit-led life, because this is our paradox.

- 6 -

The Paradox

What is a paradox? A paradox is two things that are true and make sense but are opposite of each other. Our lives are a paradox. This is how we can describe being a sinner saved by grace and living in a holy pursuit. We, ourselves, are a paradox; each of us is an unfinished masterpiece. Ephesians 2:10 says, "For we are His [God's] workmanship, created in Christ Jesus for good works, which God prepared beforehand that we should walk in them."

Every reference in the Old Testament that mentions workmanship is concerned with the skill and quality of the temple, garments, or something that was made by craftsmen. Chapters 6 through 8 of First Kings specifically cover in fine detail the splendor of Solomon's temple. The temple was the place God's people came to worship Him, and it was where God's presence lived for a time in history. When we find the word workmanship in the New Testament, we see something different. First, we find reference to our workmanship and how we build our lives or make decisions. Second, we see the

Lords workmanship, referring to how we are created in Christ Jesus.

Now that Jesus has died on the cross and overcome sin for us, we can have a close relationship with God, even when we mess up. After Jesus died and was resurrected from the dead, He promised the disciples that the Holy Spirit would come to help them live according to Kingdom culture, by overcoming sin and fulfill the commands of loving God and loving people (Acts 1:4-5). In Acts 2 we read that the Holy Spirit visited the early Christians, and He has been present with the church ever since. So, now that we have the Holy Spirit available to us, God can fill our hearts and our minds. We are now the temple!

Truly, as we are told in Ephesians 2:10, we are God's workmanship. It is most important that we take care of ourselves now so that we get to be the ones who carry the presence of God. Even though life changes things, we must take care of our bodies, our thoughts, and our emotions; and when we reach a certain age, it's important we begin to care about others as well, seeing that they, too, have been chosen by God to accomplish something special in their families and in their communities.

The word workmanship is kind of an old word these days, but the idea still rings true. Workmanship is a piece of work that generally has to do with an action: act, to fashion, furnish, bring forth, to do or to make.[1] I love what we can discover when we look at a modern version of the word workmanship and that is, masterpiece. You are a masterpiece!

Historically speaking, the word masterpiece means a piece of work that meets a specific standard and leads its viewers to the artist. This is our purpose as Christians: to live in such a way, at a specific standard set in the Bible, that others are drawn to Jesus Christ. We are His workmanship, and the choices we make reflect Jesus as our Lord and Savior. Matthew 5:16 says, "Let your light so shine before men, that they may see your good works and glorify your Father in heaven." In addition, 1 Peter 2:12 tells us to have "your conduct honorable among the Gentiles, that when they speak against you as evil-doers, they may, by your good works which they observe, glorify God in the day of visitation."

Jesus talked about this tension and so did Paul the apostle, so the concept must be one we should understand for our own lives. Even though we are not perfect we can still see the work of salvation in our lives. And just because we are still a work in progress does not mean we aren't a masterpiece, though we feel that paradoxical tension. We are still valuable to the Kingdom of God, and we are still able to function in real life as Christians by bringing the presence of God to the people around us and bringing glory to God.

When we are in the Ready! season of our lives, we will only see part of the dream; usually we don't see how hard we will have to train or how much we will have to change to reach our goal or to accomplish the vision. When we have all the details, we also have the opportunity to try to make it all happen ourselves, instead of trusting that the Lord will cause all things to work together for good. (Romans 8:28) I have found many of my peers, myself included, are all "doers." If there is a job in sight that will move us forward, we will figure out how to get it done. We will consider most of the ways to make something happen, staying up late, crying, and gritting or grinding our teeth. But, what if there was a better way—one that through those late nights and tears of loss or fear our foundation is love? The Author and Artist of our lives is the one who will see us through to completion, rather than our positive thoughts and our "get-it-together-ness." Philippians 1:6 says "that He who has begun a good work in you will complete it until the day of Jesus Christ." Our Creator will not leave us nor forsake us, since we are His prize workmanship.

We can genuinely want to do God's will, even when we don't have all of life figured out and even though we mess up. The problem isn't that we try to figure out how to make His plans happen, the problem is we try to take control of the plans. Imagine taking a paintbrush out of the artists hands and altering his or her painting.

The Sistine Chapel

Have you heard of the great works of art painted by Michelangelo on the ceiling of the Sistine Chapel in the early 1500s? The pope of his day asked him to paint the ceiling of the chapel in Vatican City in Rome, Italy.[2] Michelangelo wasn't even really a painter; he was actually a sculptor. I think this story is a great illustration of the word masterpiece, and we can draw some great conclusions too!

The painting project was so great that Michelangelo invited his friends who were painters to help him on this project, but seeing that no two painters paint alike, he eventually sent them home. Two artists can have the same vision. They can have the same colors and be told what to paint, but their unique expression through their artistic work will shine through and the results will be different.

Multiple influences (or artists) exist in our world today. Some of these are education, background, financial status, how long we have been a Christian, what job we have, whether or not we are single, our ethnicity, what we wear, who our mentors are, and the list goes on! However, we do not have to be defined by our function or our surroundings, by our culture or our experiences. We are defined by the One who created us.

Throughout the Bible we are told stories of people who did incredible things because they understood who they were and who their God was. We have to think about who we are in Christ, instead of who we are told that we are by others. You, my friend, are a masterpiece!

Michelangelo was a great choice to accomplish the task of painting the chapel because he had knowledge of the Bible and Catholic doctrine. He was able to create a masterpiece because he had the master plan. In our lives, it is the same with God. He created life, so we can trust Him with ours even when things get messy.

When Michelangelo was in the middle of the project, he noticed that mold was beginning to grow on older parts of the painting. The paint mixture was compromised. He had to start all over by removing the mold and the paint. A friend of his created a different plaster mixture that included a solution that would resist mold.[3] With this new mixture Michelangelo continued and finished the masterpiece.

The conclusion we can draw here, no pun intended, is that in our lives we will sin, and the sin will grow like a mold unless we allow God to remove it from our lives. We were not designed to live a compromised life. We were not created to live with a Kingdom mind-set only some of the time. We were intended from the beginning to live our lives by following the leading of the Holy Spirit all of the time. Sin keeps us from holiness; it keeps us from being clean and being a clear picture of God's goodness. Instead, there are parts of our hearts and minds that lack self-control and keep us living comfortable lives, harboring unforgiveness or lies that keep us loyal to fear. But then God steps in.

God sent His only Son to die on the cross for our sins. His blood was shed to cover our iniquities. A new solution was provided, a new ingredient was added to the mixture of life to help us resist sin and continue to live a life following the Lord. Isn't that incredible?

To this day, many people know Michelangelo's name because of his masterpiece in the Sistine Chapel. My sincere question to you is, how many people know the name Jesus Christ because of the masterpiece that is you?

The Dot-to-Dot

As children we learn basic skills such as drawing lines and connecting them. We are given a piece of paper that had numbers and dots all over it, in an unorganized fashion, or so it seems. Then we are handed a pencil and told to draw a line from number one to number two. We continue on until we reach the highest number and then see the image that the sequence of lines and numbers created. Yes, a dot-to-dot isn't quite the masterpiece that the Sistine Chapel is, yet we can draw some conclusions out of that illustration as well.

Our job is to follow the numbers as the Holy Spirit leads us. We will know what to do next, once we accomplish the first task. Living through the Ready! Get set! Go! seasons and learning to trust the artist will eventually result in a finished piece of work.

Now, if you're like me, you might read Ephesians 2:10 and ask different questions in the Get Set! season of an area in your life. Let's read it again: "For we are His workmanship, created in Christ Jesus for good works, which God prepared beforehand that we should walk in them." After reading this verse, I tend to ask: How do I do these good works if I don't know everything? How do I do these good works when I don't completely know what I am doing? How do I know I am doing it right?

I get the same feeling when I read Jeremiah 1:6 when the prophet says, "I am a youth," meaning untrained and inexperienced. This is where we have to trust that God is leading us through experiences, as we continue to be responsible with what is on our schedules and care for the people in our lives with excellence. When these questions come, we must not let anything define us, including our questions, except our Lord Jesus Christ who leads us.

We don't have to be overwhelmed with our weaknesses, imperfections, or shortcomings. It's not our job to complete us. It's God's job to complete us; and until we die, we are always in the process of being made. Two things we can remember when we mess up, in any season of our lives:

1. *We aren't done, until we are done.* Don't give up! Proverbs 24:16 says "the wicked shall fall by calamity." Calamity is misery or distress resulting from a disastrous event.[4] Let's keep our faith when we don't understand and when life is painful. Let's minimize our complaining and speak faith-filled words into our lives, without minimizing our pain or need for healing. As children, when we scraped our knees, we cried hard but could get help. The same is true today for our broken hearts. We can cry and position ourselves for restoration at the same time. You can live through painful experiences; and though your tear-stained cheeks may be raw, you will be whole at the end of it because that is what the grace and mercy of our Lord Jesus Christ does for us.

2. *God is not done, until we are done!* When we mess up it is important that we repent as soon as we realize our error. Changing requires reading the Bible and allowing it to change the way we think. It requires submitting our emotions (no matter how strong) to the Word of God. Paul says in Philippians, "being confident of this, that he who began a good work in you will carry it on to completion until the day of Christ Jesus" (1:6 NIV). So change the channel, unfollow or unsubscribe from you-know-who, and turn off the iPad—get rid of anything that is a stumbling block to your transformation—and, instead, turn on worship music, read your Bible, and ask the Holy Spirit for help to change the scene of your life.

Unfinished Masterpiece

Each of us is a masterpiece; and though we are a work in progress, we are still of great value, can still be appreciated, and can still function and be used by God to accomplish His will for our lives. We can do what God asks us to do in each season. In fact, we will do very well by not worrying about other seasons. Matthew says in his Gospel, "Therefore I tell you, do not worry about your life, what you will eat or drink; or about your body, what you will wear. Is not life more than food, and the body more than clothes?" (6:25 NIV). We need to plan our lives and dream big dreams, but we are not asked to worry. In fact, we are specifically instructed to not worry! When we believe we are a masterpiece, then we truly know who we are in Christ and understand God's promises. As an unfinished masterpiece, we are imperfect persons who are accomplishing good works for a perfect God in an imperfect world! Note that the Bible says:

We are blessed! (Psalms 1; 119:1-3)
We will have peace. (Psalm 119:165)
We will have joy. (Psalm 16:11; John 15:11)
We are overcomers! (1 John 5:4)
We will receive wisdom when we ask in faith. (James 1:5)
We will be satisfied/content/fulfilled. (Psalm 107:9)
We are satisfied in our souls; that is, our mind, will, and
    emotions. (Psalm 63:5)
We are continually growing and being challenged in our
    faith in God. (Romans 5:3-4; James 1:3)
We are built/constructed/created by God. (Ephesians
    2:10)
We will be full of the Spirit, given what we need at the
    time that we need it. (1 Corinthians 4:6-13)

And again,
We are blessed! (James 1:25)

We are indeed a masterpiece; and if we walk and talk (two very practical things) like one, the purposes of God will be perfected in our lives. We won't be perfect, but God's purposes will be perfected. That is so powerful! God has prepared good works for us, and it is our purpose in life to do them with excellence. These works are the influence we have through practical decision-making. Works are the demonstration of a real faith. Here are some of the good works God has prepared for us:

We can hear the Lord.
We can know our calling.
We can live a purpose-filled life.

We can obey the Lord.
We can accomplish what He is asking of us in each
season of our lives.
We can strengthen a weak area.
We can love the person who is annoying, offensive,
and unlovely.
We can have peace in a dysfunctional family.
We can overcome the enemy in our minds.
We can think faith-filled thoughts.
We can be leaders by living according to the standard
the Bible sets and inviting others to do the same.
We can move forward in the promises of God.

Because you, my friend, are a masterpiece:

You can bring glory to God and be imperfect.
You can contribute in the church and be imperfect.
You can have a family and be imperfect.
You can be a good steward of your health and
finances and be imperfect.
You can get an education and be imperfect.
You can see a broken relationship restored, and be
imperfect.

Because you are a masterpiece you were created to do these things well! You can do all of them and still be imperfect! Now, that we know we are a work in progress, let's talk about going to the Bible for the answers to the questions we may ask as we grow.

The Bible Doesn't Say That

Going to the Word to get answers for all of life's questions can be confusing and, if I am honest, even discouraging at times. The Bible is not a dictionary; it's a love story with hidden treasures; and unless you read it over and over again, you won't know what to look for or where to search for the treasures. For example, when we ask ourselves, "What does kindness mean?" we can go online or flip through the pages of a dictionary and find a list of words that start with the letter K. Now, we find the word kindness, and next to the word are little letters and punctuation that tell us it's a noun. Then we see the definitions: (1) "the quality or state of being kind;" (2) a kind deed: Favor; and (3) "Affection."[1] Then, when we decide we want to be kind, we can simply think, "Show affection." There it is! Our question is answered in black and white. But the Bible is not like that.

You see, the Bible is written in black and white; and, in many Bibles, red, when Jesus is speaking. But life is not black and white; instead, it is more of an ombré of gray. So how do we find the answers to the questions we have in life when life is difficult and so is understanding the Bible? First, we must understand more about our salvation, which is why I began this book sharing some thoughts on success and salvation. Let's dig in.

Three in One

God made humans with three distinct parts: (1) Body: our brain, bones, muscles, skin, hormones, and so forth; (2) Soul: our mind (thoughts), our will (natural desires), and our emotions; (3) Spirit: the center of our being that should lead us, despite our natural desires, thoughts, or emotions. Today, many cultures describe the spirit as the "heart".

When we sin all three of these parts are affected, and we see the effects in some places sooner than others, which means we need a Lord and Savior for each of these parts. You see, when we ask Jesus to be our Lord and Savior, the process of sanctification begins, which means we are continually being saved because we sin all of the time. Hopefully less and less, but still . . . .

The first time we ask Jesus to be the Lord and Savior of our lives, He washes our spirit immediately and we are made new! Second Corinthians 5 says, "This means that anyone who belongs to Christ has become a new person. The old life is gone; a new life has begun!" (verse 17 NLT). In other words, we are forgiven of our mistakes, and the sin that has held us back from experiencing the presence of God no longer has a hold on us. We can experience God's power in our lives today!

Then, every day and every moment, until we die, our souls will need continual saving. This is sanctification. We aren't perfect, and we need Jesus to change us as we get to know Him (through reading our Bibles). This change was explained in chapter 3 and is heavily talked about in the book of Romans by the apostle Paul.

I think if God set people free immediately from their bad habits, they wouldn't be strong enough in their discipline and character to continue living a free life and would return to their sin. That would make matters worse, because knowing Christ's power but not having a disciplined soul is the devil's playground for shame. The devil will condemn us every time we mess up, and if we don't strengthen and discipline ourselves to learn how to get back up (through Christ), then the weight of our sin (like gravity) will pull us down again. It is not natural for a sinner to understand righteous matters. We must continually strengthen the sanctification process by studying the Bible regularly.

Finally, when we die and go to heaven, we will receive a new body. Since it will be a perfect body, I am thinking it will be one that doesn't require exercise, naps, or even coffee, unfortunately.

Until that day comes, we need to study the Bible to find Jesus's answers, the red words that stand out against the gray questions. Here is one way to do that:

Step 1: Make an appointment to meet with God.

Put the one-on-one meeting on your calendar at a time that you know will work for you—on any day of the week that fits your schedule—when you won't be interrupted. During a lunch break at school, when the children are napping, or just before bedtime works well for me. Before I actually go to this appointment, I like to get some things on my to-do list checked off, such as making coffee for myself and feeding my children their breakfast. Otherwise, I'll be too distracted, thinking about what I am putting on hold in order to spend time with God.

Step 2: Prepare for your appointment with God.

- Write down one or two situations in which you need God. Be honest!
- Write down three things in your life for which you are thankful.
- Download a Bible app (many are free of charge) or purchase a physical Bible that you will commit to read.
- Find a Bible reading plan that you want to follow. A plan that covers a topic for which you are looking for answers could be the most helpful.
- Have a notebook ready to fill up!

Step 3: At your first appointment, sit down and turn off your phone and leave it in another room.

Review the situations you wrote down previously and pray. Ask God to help you find direction in your life, and ask for His help to show you the way. Next, look at the list of things you are thankful for and pray God protects the blessings you already have. Then create for yourself another appointment with God. Remember to add it to your calendar.

Step 4: At your second appointment follow the instructions provided in your Bible plan.

After reading your Bible ask yourself the below questions. Begin to get comfortable with silence. Even if you have worship music playing in the background, focus your thoughts.

- What is the situation that I am reading about?
- What happened to the people in this reading?
- How did God treat these people? (Do I need to read more in order to know this answer?)
- Based on God's actions, what can I learn about Him? (Do I need to read more to understand?)

Write the answers to these questions under your list of situations and blessings. Pray again, asking for clarity in your life and for protection over the good things God has given you. Continue to think about these observations throughout your day.

Step 5: Continue to set appointments with God and live by principle.

What does "living by principle" mean? Living by principle is living in a way that produces a specific result. Think about math principles. If you do the steps, you get the right answer. The same thing applies to your relationship with God. If you have repeatedly experienced God's love, you'll love God and love people naturally. You will want others to know how incredible His love is. Practically, examples of living by principle includes: choosing forgiveness, honoring authority, or not flaking out when you could be serving others in your family or church. You'll find the grace to care authentically for those around you at work, school, and home. You can start living by principle today, but a principled life is built over time as you learn the principles in the Book. Remember God is your source.

Listen, friends: God doesn't mind if you need to reschedule because you feel overwhelmed with life. Just make sure you reschedule! He is the Author of life, so I highly recommend that you check in with Him first every day, before your usual social platforms or business e-mails. Every time you meet with God, pray and ask Him to reveal Himself. Then read the Bible to answer the questions above.

The Bible Doesn't Say That

We are all facing situations as we are reading the Bible, and it seems as if the Bible doesn't have answers to some of the complicated problems we experience in life. Heavy questions such as "Why do bad things happen to good people?" or "Why did God let sin enter the world in the first place?" or every day questions including, "What should I do with my life?", "What kind of person should I date?", and a more recent debatable question,"Whom should I vote for?" The Bible doesn't answer those questions directly. But if we study further, we will find that answers to the "what should I do?" questions of life are available to us. The Holy Spirit is always faithful to use the stories in the Bible to guide us, but we have to know the stories first.

Every story has a beginning, middle, and end. This is true for my life and your life; in fact there are multiple beginnings, middles, and ends. To break it down further, every day has these moments included in them. Every morning is the beginning of a new day, every evening is the end, and what happens in-between is the middle. For the most part we can decide what happens with the beginning, the middle, and the end of our day. We should decide to read the Bible to get to know how God treats people. When something happens in our day that we didn't choose, we can still get through it. Why? Because we have been keeping our appointments with God and reading our Bibles, learning to live by principle. Reading the Bible doesn't give us answers to our biggest questions right away. In fact, the power from reading our Bible comes from the practical discipline of studying it regularly. For our story to be powerful, it must include studying God's story.

The Elements of a Story

Every story contains five elements. When we unpack these elements, we understand the story better. They are: characters, setting, plot, conflict, and resolution. These elements are found in the Bible as well. In fact, when you consider story elements, there are layers and layers of knowledge to study in the Bible. When we read our Bible, we can ask some of these questions:

Characters

- What are the character's names, and what do their names mean?
- What are their personalities and character like?
- How do they think?
- How are they feeling? (How does their culture influence these feelings?)
- What choices are they making? (How does their culture influence their choices? Or, are they aware of cultural ex-

pectations, and obeying the Lord instead? If so, what is at risk?)
- Do they know God?
- What helped them make the choice to obey God?

Setting
- Where is the story happening? (city, farm, mountain, valley, desert, on a boat in a sea, etc.)
- What is life like there? (Consider: politics, education, family traditions, etc.)

Plot
- What is happening in the chapter you are reading? Is it good or bad?
- How are God's people acting?
- Think: should I pray the prayers they are praying?
- Think: should I copy the attitudes and choices they are making?

Conflict
- Does a problem exist in this chapter?
- If so, what is the problem?
- Is the problem an internal or external one? (Internal problems include our thoughts, attitudes, and emotions. External problems include things such as money, the words we use, cultural structures, or actions we take or don't take.)

Resolution
- Is the problem solved? (Do I need to read more to find out?)
- How is the problem solved?

- What choices did the people make to fix the conflict?
- Did those choices work?
- What choices did God make to remedy the conflict?
- What is the main point the author is communicating about the passage?
- How can I apply what I am learning to my life today?

Notice that you won't be able to completely answer these questions after sitting down in one appointment with God. Furthermore, some answers aren't a simple yes or no—not black and white—there are layers in the Word, just as in life. Our God is very capable of controlling a world that is ombré grey, and He so believes in us that we can live a life of following the Spirit because of the red blood Jesus shed when He died on the cross. We can live red in a world of gray. We can live according to God's ways in a culture filled with people who are living however they desire.

Set another appointment and continue to read the Bible to look for the answers to life's questions. You'll be amazed at what the Holy Spirit helps you recognize as you read.

Write these two questions on a sticky note and put them on the mirror in your bathroom or inside your Bible to think about and answer daily:

1. Based on what I am reading, what have I learned about God? Do any of these facts match my life now?
2. If yes, how does that help? What is inspiring about what I have learned? If no, keep reading or perhaps go where the Bible reading plan leads (the part of the Bible you have been reading may not address your situation). That is totally fine. Just stay disciplined to read the Bible, and set another

appointment to do an online search for the topic you wish to study and the appropriate Bible verses.

Why set appointments to find these things? Because setting appointments usually means something has become a priority. Setting appointments in our calendar makes the vision a strategy. The Bible does cover everything we may face in life; however, since today's culture is different from the culture in which the Bible was originally written, we need to read the Book, connect with other Christians, and follow the leading of the Holy Spirit to find our answers. We can live righteously when we understand who our God is, how He thinks about us, and what He desires for our lives. As you partner with the Holy Spirit, your ideas can become reality.

God loves you! Start reading your Bible every day; read about the people He called His own and how well they were treated, even through hardships and imperfections. The practical things in your life will become powerful as you read and accept God's purpose in them.

- 8 -

Resting in the Power

Almost nine years ago my husband and I were serving at my parent's church. I was on the staff, and he was a volunteer at the highest level. We loved the people in that congregation, the youth and their staff, the parents and their children. We still do. Yet something inside us was stirring, and we started to ask God where He wanted to take us in our walk with Him. As it turns out, we were put into the position of having to choose whom we wanted to serve—the opinions of people or God's plan for our lives. I must be honest: this was the hardest decision I have ever had to make in my entire life. Marrying Trevin was an easier decision than this. Can I be honest again? Living for God is harder than just living as everyone else does. In the quiet of our first home, as there were no children yet, the walls were familiar with the voice of my prayers, and the pillows were soaked with my salty tears. The year was 2010, and we had been married for only two years, but we agreed God was moving us.

The decision to make a move was huge. Trevin was working at Costco when he asked God for a Bible verse to confirm the word he had received. And the Lord delivered. We don't necessarily need a Bible verse for every decision, but for life-altering decisions we ask God for one. He has always been so faithful to us despite our perfectionist personalities; we're both firstborn. After receiving the word from God, Trevin and I received counseling from our pastors to help us process the transition from Nampa, Idaho to Portland, Oregon, which is where we are now. In that time of counseling many seasons changed for us, including the fact that we became parents! I gave birth to a healthy baby boy, and we named him Boston Matthew. His name means "a place that is a gift from God."[1] Little did we know our son's name had a special meaning in our story, as it still does today.

During this same time period, our church entered a tumultuous season, and one of our dear elders developed a neurological disease called Lou Gehrig's Disease, also known as ALS. Because of these three very big shifts in our lives, Trevin and I stopped talking about the idea of moving; we stopped dreaming about it, and we really didn't even ask God for clarity. We put the idea "on the shelf," knowing that if moving was God's will it would happen in His timing and we would just know. We decided to put our hands to the plow and continue to be faithful with what we had been given already, to be strong support and examples in the church, and to enjoy our little boy's first year of life. Our word wasn't more important than the season in which the local body of believers found ourselves.

In 2011 we celebrated our first Christmas as a family of three in our first home. Oh, how I loved watching my little guy rolling around under the real pine branches and playing with the bells. I remember specifically just lying there looking at the lights and soaking up every moment, as I thought about the Christmas story and how much my God had changed my life when He granted salvation to me as a nine-year-old little girl. We were blessed, and we knew it.

On December 31st we decided to stay home instead of going to a New Year's party. After all, we were parents of a six-month-old and still needed to catch all the sleep we could. I put Boston in his crib, and I went to my room to sleep around 9p.m. Trevin came to bed later and also fell asleep. It was a quiet end to a year we never imagined, a year of blessing and a year of breaking.

Midnight came, and all of a sudden I was wide awake. Trevin's breathing patterned changed, and he woke up too. We both looked at our clocks, sort of confused, and asked, why are we awake right now? Trevin looked at me and said, "This is it. This is our year." I didn't even respond. I knew exactly what he meant. I hid those words in my heart as I wondered how the year would play out. I remember that moment so vividly.

The new year came: January 2012. Our church was in a season of prayer and fasting, seeking God for His direction for the year. I was sitting in the back row with my sister and her toddler while my dad shared a word with the leaders of the church. The word was this: "It's time to cross over!" The text was from the book of Exodus, when Moses was leading the children of Israel out of Egypt into the promised land. And there it was: the pastor confirming Trevin's word with his own words. I continued to hold each moment in my heart, and we emailed our pastors to ask if we could continue our pastoral counseling on the idea of transition with two great leaders who supported me during my years of Bible college.[2]

So, there we were, two years later, with the word confirmed by our pastor and two other mentors guiding us in our transition. Our lives had changed dramatically, and we were better for it.

At the end of our prayer and fasting season my parents, the pastors of our church, invited us into their office and asked us what we thought God had in store for us for the year 2012. Trevin looked at me and said, "Well, here we go!" I just cried, and so did my mom. We talked briefly about the timeline and how my dad would like us to go about transitioning our responsibilities to those who were on our teams; and we did our best, loving on our friends, saving our money, researching cost of living in Portland, and raising our firstborn.

Fast forward to May 24th, 2012, Trevin was in his truck, my dad was driving our moving truck, and my mom and I drove with the baby in our car to Vancouver, Washington to an apartment just outside of Portland, Oregon. We unloaded and unpacked, cried, and unpacked some more. The weather was cold but bright, and our apartment had new paint and new carpet, which I was grateful for, even though the apartment and streets were ghetto. We made it our home. During that month we got to know the area, visited our new church, made friends, and got reacquainted with individuals I knew from college who were now married with children themselves. When Trevin wasn't working at Costco, our schedule was filled with dinners and coffee appointments and exploring the area. Then it happened.

Only a few weeks had gone by when our new church was hosting a leadership team meeting, and we were invited to join. Trevin and I grabbed one of the executive pastors and asked if this was even appropriate. We weren't leading anyone; we had just moved there. We had no fruit to show in this new season and nothing to prove—just us, our baby, and our choice to move there. The pastor looked at us and said, "Well, you're leaders, aren't you?" To which we smiled and replied, "Yes, we are leaders." We do have influence.

We were excited to be at this meeting; but, of course, we didn't know what was going to happen or who would be there. We were just happy to be with people who love to serve the people of God. These were our people. We took Boston to childcare and got to our seats, somewhere in the middle and kind of on the right side of the room, but definitely nowhere that was special. It was just the two of us, worshipping and hoping God would help us settle into this new land He had led us to. It was during this worship service that the pastor of this congregation, walked on stage and stood at the pulpit with his eyes closed. He was listening for the Holy Spirit to give him direction. He didn't say a word. He didn't move. He just focused on the Lord.

This particular moment of waiting on the Lord is seared in my mind, like a long, drawn out pause of time ticking slowly. There was silence. Then the pastor broke the silence with four short words: "You have crossed over!" My breath was taken away from me as my tears started to pour for probably the thousandth time in the last two years. With my hands over my mouth and my eyes shut tight, I remember saying "We did it!" We obeyed God, and it was hard.

Is there an area of your life where God is asking you to obey? Is it difficult to obey? If so, why?

Learning To Rest

When God gives us a word, it's important we rest in His timing, rely on those with spiritual authority in our lives, and never respond alone.

Resting in the power means resting in the knowledge that God's plans will happen when He is ready. Until then, we stay faithful to accomplish the responsibilities with which we have already been entrusted. This includes our physical health, finances, jobs, serving regularly at church, attending college, and our relationships.

Our job is to accomplish those things with a high standard. That can include such things as not acquiring debt, finding a good job (it doesn't have to be a fancy one, just not an illegal one), working to live (your job might not be your passion, but let it finance your passions), treating people with kindness, getting good at running errands, forgiving, and showing mercy. It means showing up on time and keeping your word when you make a promise.

Resting in the power means not avoiding the stuff in the corner of your room that needs to be dealt with. Resting in the power means taking care of what God has given to us and letting Him take care of what is coming to us.

God gives us great responsibilities in our work, our families, and our communities. We must take care how we talk *about* people and how we talk to people. We must take care of our homes and our places of work or education.

Resting in the power means trusting that God will make the seasons change in His timing. It means controlling our thoughts, words, and attitudes; and not allowing them to wander until the day the seasons change. Resting means not rushing transitions.

Resting is feeling all of the emotions but not letting them change your mind or your actions. Resting in the power is an active trust to believe in more but steward what you have. It means reading your Bible until you understand and until you hear God.

As we make decisions about the plans God has for us, we have to consider two things: (1) God's moral will and (2) God's sovereign will. These two ideas are very complex, but we can simplify them. God's moral will is exact; it's a list of dos and donts. For example: lying, murdering, racism, pornography, and committing adultery are not acceptable. God's sovereign will allows us to make our own decisions as we learn and understand the Bible. For example: deciding on a career or a college. A practical guideline is to submit applications to locations for which you are qualified. It's OK to choose a place you think you would enjoy and make great pay for your age and experience. God's sovereignty covers all of our choices. He is so much in control that He can allow us imperfect humans to make choices, and each choice can lead to an understanding of His love for us. As we rest we must trust. As we rest God will see us through.

Love Is the Foundation for Powerful Living

One Saturday night I woke up in the middle of the night from a bad dream. I remembered all the friends I hadn't seen in a long time and some friends I had lost touch with since moving to Portland seven years earlier. I woke up grieving the loss, and I felt so far from God. I didn't regret our choice to move, I just missed some people and wondered if they missed me back; and I recognized for some they probably didn't, which is why my heart was aching.

That next morning I woke up, and instead of sleeping in, I went to church to reaffirm my commitment to the Lord and this new church family. During worship, the Lord brought to my mind Romans 8:31-39:

> What then shall we say to these things? If God is for us, who can be against us? He who did not spare His own Son, but delivered Him up for us all, how shall He not with Him also freely give us all things? Who shall bring a charge against God's elect? It is God who justifies. Who is he who condemns? It is Christ who died, and furthermore is also risen, who is even at the right hand of God, who also makes intercession for us. Who shall separate us from the love of Christ? Shall tribulation, or distress, or persecution, or famine, or nakedness, or peril, or sword? As it is written:

> "For Your sake we are killed all day long;
> We are accounted as sheep for the slaughter."

> Yet in all these things we are more than conquerors through Him who loved us. For I am persuaded that neither death nor life, nor angels nor principalities nor powers, nor things present nor things to come, nor height nor depth, nor any other created thing, shall be able to separate us from the love of God which is in Christ Jesus our Lord.

When we spend time reading the Bible every day, and we need it to comfort us, it will!

94

A Picture of God's Love

Picture yourself on the edge of a cliff. Across the canyon is another cliff, and your goal is there—that healthy family lifestyle, healing from heartache, the power to forgive, starting a business, growing a team—it's on the other side, out of our reach. When we make decisions that help us reach those goals, we are building a bridge across the gorge. Each step we take is a step of faith, believing that we are closer to the goal than when we started. But how can we be so sure we are getting closer? We can be sure because the love of God is the foundation of the bridge. His love bridges the gap from one side to the other.

Just as Romans 8:39 says, "nor height nor depth . . . shall be able to separate us from the love of God," rest assured we can rely on the love of God to be the solid foundation for each step we take on the bridge we build.

We should focus on not just moving but moving in the right direction. That is progress. No matter how dark the situation, the Bible says in Psalm 119:105 that His word is a "lamp to my feet and a light to my path." You can still make progress! And a little progress in an entire lifetime is better than no progress! A life lived focusing on obeying the voice of God is a life that will progress.

If you are looking to live a powerful life in the practical areas, rest in the power of the Bible, trusting that each step forward is supported by His love and nothing can separate you from that solid foundation. The more you read the Bible, the more you will see how much God loves His people and how well He treats them. Actually, you will find that mistake after mistake, dream after dream, God is present being faithful to humanity, and to you, through all of it. He believes in you. Jesus wants to be your Lord.

Do you want to live a life that is effective? Work hard to accomplish the responsibilities you have on your calendar right now, believe God for opportunities to be effective, like my husband did when he had the opportunity to serve others in Japan, trust in His perfect timing, and read your Bible every day. Together, we can spread this idea of living powerfully and practically—living a life that is surrendered to Jesus our Lord and Savior, the expert of living by faith (Hebrews 12:2)—by allowing the Bible to shape our everyday decisions.

Start with the decision to read the Book.

Discussion Questions

Grab a coffee, a pen and journal.

Chapter One

1. According to the primary definition of power (effective), do you think you can make decisions that are powerful? Why?

2. What does the secondary definition of power (influence and control) mean to you? Have you chosen to let God have power over your life?

3. Do you know the promises God has made toward you?

4. What promise from the Bible do you need to be a reality for you right now?

Chapter Two

1. What retired situations from your past are pressuring you to be loyal to the old you—the you who existed before you knew about Jesus the Savior?

2. What lies take away your power to represent Jesus the Lord with confidence?

3. What experiences influence you to think that you are not made new in Christ Jesus? (2 Corinthians 5:17)

4. What experiences allow you to think that you are not loved? (Romans 5:8)

Chapter Three

1. Review steps to change:

The first step is to give up control of how we think the change process should look and give up control of how the end result will look.

The second step to experiencing change is rehearsing the stories or inspiring verses that you read from the Bible, and let it change our perspective.

As our perspective is changed, we must plan to act differently, which is step three.

Finally, step four, stay committed to the process of change and don't stop. Even if it's difficult, even if you mess up, and when life gets busy.

2. How can we be successful in each step towards change?

3. What is the Holy Spirits role in our lives as we pursue change in our lives?

Chapter Four

1. What can we learn from how Jesus responded to temptation?

2. What is twisted truth?

3. What are some ways Satan tries to distract or deceive us? Knowing these things, how can we prepare ourselves to respond the same way Jesus did?

4. How do you hear God?

5. What are some things you can do to get the Word inside of you?

Chapter Five

1. What dream are you currently fulfilling?

2. What goal have you accomplished that was once just an idea?

3. After accomplishing a goal, how do you feel about reaching for another goal?

4. How does knowing the Bible help you reach a goal?

4. What does God think about your goals?

Chapter Six

1. Are you in a Ready! Season? What can you do well right now, knowing you are in a Ready! season?

2. Are you in a Get Set! season? What can you do now to prepare yourself for the next season?

3. Are you in a Go! season? Did it turn out how you thought it would? What is different?

4. What can you do well in this (or any) season of your life, even though you are not perfect?

Chapter Seven

1. Open your calendar and schedule your first three appointments with God.

2. Set reminders ahead of time so that you are prepared for those appointments.

3. What is important in your life that you would like to study from the Bible?
*In the appendix I list books my mom used and websites I currently use to study with. Start with those as you search. If you don't have a topic to search consider learning more about one of these current issues in todays world:
    Abuse
    Authority

Compassion
Education and Knowledge
Having big dreams
Healthy families and how to have one
Identity
Owing people money
Racism
Refugees
Sexuality
Success

Chapter Eight

1. Describe a time it was difficult to obey God's Word? What made it difficult? What helped you make the right choice?

2. Resting in the power means being faithful until God's timing is revealed. What are some ways you can be faithful when you are waiting on God to open a door or answer a prayer in your life?

3. What are somethings you would like to do in the future, knowing you can live an effective life?

4. Open your calendar and schedule three more appointments with God.

5. Plan to go to church regularly and add that to your schedule.

Appendix

Kyushu Christ Disaster Relief Center

Kyushu Christ Disaster Support Center / Headquarters
Hours: 9:00-17: 00 (closed Sunday and Monday)
Tel. and Fax: 092-873-6235
Email: kyusyuchristdrc@gmail.com

Books my mom used for studying the Bible:

Strong's Concordance
Bible Dictionary
Joyce Meyer and Marilyn Hickey Resources

Websites I love to resource when I study the Bible:

1. BibleGateway.com
Menu > Study > Passage Study, Key Word Study, or
    Top-ical Index
2. BibleStudyTools.com.
Menu > Study or Tools

Beginning a relationship with Jesus:

It's really important to me that you know Jesus Christ loves you and if you haven't begun a relationship with Him, can I implore you to start? He died on a cross to bring you out of a life of sin and confusion and to give you a new life. One that will be effective. As you read the Bible and surrender to His ways, you will begin to change and eventually thrive. It may even influence the friends and family around you and they may also begin to thrive. If you have not asked Jesus to be your Lord and Savior, please consider this prayer as a conversation starter:

Jesus,
I am learning about You as Lord and as Savior.
(Feel free to talk to Him about how your life is going.)
Thank You for helping me to find You.
I am sorry for trying to live life without You as my Lord and Savior.
Please forgive me.
I want You in my life.
Help me to understand the Bible,
which teaches me how to live,
so that my choices honor You every day.
I believe in You, Jesus.
From now on, You are in charge of everything in my life.
Help me to remember that truth every day,
regardless of how I feel.
Help me to live a life that pleases You, Lord.
Thank you.
Amen.

My friend, if you said these words genuinely for the first time, or again, I am so proud of you. This choice to become a Christian is the most powerful choice you can make in your life. Welcome to the family of believers that spans all across the world! You may be asking, "OK, what do I do now?" Can I encourage you to find a church? Why? Well, we read the Bible to know God, but we understand the Bible by belonging to a Church (family.)

Why find a Church:

Finding a church to join can be uncomfortable, trying something new always is. However, finding a church is critical to your relationship with Jesus. The church is His body. The expression of Jesus comes from the people who gather regularly in his name. To know Jesus one must know His body (the people,) that is the way God designed it. It is also critical to be in community with a healthy church so that you can understand the Bible better. One person on their own cannot understand all the complexities of the Word. We learn best from each other. You can begin your search by looking online or ask a Christian friend or coworker to help you find the churches in your area.

What to look for when finding a Church:

1. *Families.* Are there are a good number of families at this church? If so, that says something good. Even if you don't have children, look around. Multigenerational churches usually have solid people you can trust, people who have wisdom to share from their past experiences. A church has a bright future

if there are children being raised there. This is a sign that the church cares about the health of its community. In my opinion, after leading children's church for more than nineteen years, the best churches have the best children's ministries.

2. *Worship.* Is the music inspiring? When you hear the sounds and sing the words, do you seem to feel closer to God? This is called presence-driven worship.

3. *Speaking.* When the preacher stands in front of the congregation and shares a thought, is the thought from the Bible? Is the message filled with hope even if it talks about the problems we face in life today? The Bible should be the main focus of the message time.

Note: there is no such thing as a perfect church, and experiences will vary based on culture and demographics. But if you find a congregation who "loves God and loves people," as Jesus commanded, that church is a good place to start your life as a new Christian.

Ready! Get Set! Go!

Scriptures from the Bible to support David's experiences in each Ready! Get Set! Go! season (from chapter 5). All of these are taken from the life of David:

A. Ready!

- God will call you. (1 Samuel 16:12-13)
- God will point you out to yourself so that you notice how important and valuable you are. (1 Samuel 16:12-13)
- Your heart motives will begin to be exposed. (1 Samuel 17:28 & 29)

- You will be tempted to become distracted by things that may seem "necessary" to the natural mind but may not match a Kingdom mind-set. (1 Samuel 17:37-39)
- You will be discouraged to not even try and just give up. (1 Samuel 17:33)
- God will show you what abilities and victories you already have. (1 Samuel 17:37)
- The goal, the calling, will seem impossible. (1 Samuel 17:33, 42-47)
- You might feel a "righteous anger" at the challenges or hurdles you face (1 Samuel 17:26). (Righteous anger is that anger that comes from understanding God's ways and knowing the challenges that oppose the truth.)
- Your focus should be on the goal and staying humble with your technique. (1 Samuel 17:39-40)
- You might see no change in your day-to-day responsibilities except that you now notice that God has His eye on you for something special. (1 Samuel 17:15-20)
- You must remember the Lord in times of pressure and opposition. (1 Samuel 17:45-47)
- You will need to develop a trust that God will position you in the right time to Get Set! (1 Samuel 16:16-23)

B. Get Set!

- Education & training become valuable here. (1 Samuel 16:18)
- Opposition and misunderstandings begin to take place. (1 Samuel 17:28-30)

- You begin to recognize the tools and abilities God revealed and developed in you during the Ready! stage. (1 Samuel 17:40)
- (Though there will be resistance) opposition will not be able to stand against you. (1 Samuel 17:51 & 52)
- You will find true friendships. (1 Samuel 18:1-3)
- You'll be persecuted. (1 Samuel 18:10-11)
- People may have issues with you for no reason other than you are advancing in life. (1 Samuel 17:29; 19:4 & 5)
- When people begin to see your growth, some will not like it. (1Samuel 18:8 & 9)
- Allow others to share their perspective. (Wrestle with the facts, ask for prayer, get advice, do some research). (1 Samuel 20:1)
- Your moments of waiting may look like absence or be misunderstood by others (1 Samuel 20:24-26)
- The goal may look further away than before. (1 Samuel 20:41 & 42)
- You will see and feel what habits and relationships must change or go away. (The Bible defines this as "counting the cost" in Luke 14:25.) All of your responsibilities will be affected. (1 Samuel 20:42)
- You may have more questions and fewer answers than you did before. (1 Samuel 20:42)
- You will have small reminders of past victories that should challenge and encourage you to stay faithful and keep your integrity in difficult times. (1 Samuel 21:9)
- It might look like nothing, but the Lord will add to you. Do not despise the small beginnings! (1 Samuel 22:2; Zachariah 4:10)

- It's possible to get stuck. Stay focused and keep moving forward. (1 Samuel 22:4 & 5)
- Fear, doubt, and mistakes will chase you, you will have to take courage again and again. (1 Samuel 22:6-13)
- Other people's lives will look more comfortable or as if they have already achieved their God idea. (1 Samuel 23:18)
- You will have opportunities to advance the wrong way. Use self-control. (1 Samuel chapters 24 and 26)
- You will experience loss. (1 Samuel 25:1)
- God will bring you wisdom to help you continue to use self-control. (1 Samuel 25:23-35)
- Everything will be taken from you and your entire life will feel the weight of the cost, the exchange in the sacrifice. (1 Samuel 30:6) Remember: David strengthened himself in the Lord when things were painful!
- You will have to fight for what is yours! Advancement is a battle with great resistance. (1 Samuel 30:18 & 19)
- You will have opportunity to be stingy with what is yours, be generous. (1 Samual 30:26)
- Obstacles will begin to move. (1 Samuel 31)
- It is healthy to grieve when your enemies and friends fall. (2 Samuel 1:23; Proverbs 24:17)
- Earthly authority figures and mentors may change. (2 Samuel 2:8-11)
- You will be challenged to despise the small beginnings, the little successes; you'll want to give up out of frustration and despise your youth. Be encouraged! Your goal and your invitation from the Lord to accomplish this desire are not lost! (2 Samuel 2:10 & 11)

C. Go!

- We will see God's promises fulfilled. (2 Samuel 2:4)
- We will continue to be misunderstood and judged. (2 Samuel 6:16-23)
- We will need to speak our identity, address any challenges, and ignore labels. (2 Samuel 6:21 &22)We will be blessed. (2 Samuel 7:18-29)
- We will be tempted to take it easy in moments of advancement. (2 Samuel 11:1)
- We will mess up. Let's own our mistakes and get back on track! (2 Samuel Chapters 11 & 12)
- Others will be effected by our decisions; team, family, opposition, etc. (2 Samuel 12:11-14; Proverbs 29:2)
- We will have victory and complete the assignment God has chosen us for and called us to. (2 Samuel 22:32-46)
- The Lord will be glorified through your life. (2 Samuel 22:47-49)
- Continually thank the Lord for everything happening in your life. (2 Samuel 50:51)

Notes

Preface

1. Walter A. Elwell, ed., Baker's Evangelical Dictionary of Biblical Theology, s.v. "Bible, Canon of the," BibleStudyTools.com, accessed April 24, 2019, https://www.biblestudytools.com/dictionaries/bakers-evangelical-dictionary/the-bible-canon-of.html.

2. Penny Starr, "Education Expert: Removing Bible, Prayer from Public Schools Has Caused Decline," CNSNews.com, August 15, 2014, https://www.cnsnews.com/news/article/penny-starr/education-expert-removing-bible-prayer-public-schools-has-caused-decline.

3. Merriam-Webster, s.v. "faith (n.)," accessed April 12, 2019, http://www.merriam-webster.com/dictionary/faith.

Chapter 1: Power and Practical

1. "OCHA Flash Update - Japan | Kumamoto Earthquake," ReliefWeb, April 16, 2016,
https://reliefweb.int/report/japan/ocha-flash-update-japan-kumamoto-earthquake-16-april-2016.

2. Merriam-Webster, s.v. "practical (adj.)," accessed March 31, 2019, http://www.merriam-webster.com/dictionary/practical.

3. Merriam-Webster, s.v. "power (n.)," accessed February 28, 2019, http://www.merriam-webster.com/dictionary/power.

4. Merriam-Webster, s.v. "power (n.)."

Chapter 2: The Problem with Jesus, Our Lord and Savior

1. Merriam-Webster, s.v. "lord (n.)," accessed October 15, 2018, http://www.merriam-webster.com/dictionary/lord.

2. Merriam-Webster, s.v. "believe (v.)," accessed October 15, 2018, http://www.merriam-webster.com/dictionary/believe.

Chapter 4: Power Comes from His Words: How to Hear God

1. James Strong, The Strongest Strong's Exhaustive Concordance of the Bible, s.v. "sin," Greek #264, 266 (Grand Rapids, MI: Zondervan, 2001).

2. Stephanie Anderson, "How to Hear God," Andersonswife.com, February 24, 2018,
https://andersonswife.com/2018/02/24/how-to-hear-god/.

Chapter 5: Power Comes from Understanding Times and Seasons

1. When my husband was fifteen years old, his mom had her first stroke, and by the time he entered his senior year of high school, he was approved to have early release from school

to take care of her while his dad worked. Trevin's mom died during his senior year. A few months later he moved to Meridian, Idaho and visited my church where we would soon meet and our love story would begin to be written.

2. Beth Moore, Esther: It's Tough Being a Woman (Nashville: Lifeway, 2008).

3. Merriam-Webster, s.v. "anoint (v.)," accessed October 15, 2018, http://www.merriam-webster.com/dictionary/anoint.

4. James Strong, The Strongest Strong's Exhaustive Concordance of the Bible, s.v. "anoint," Hebrew #4882; Greek #218 (Grand Rapids, MI: Zondervan, 2001).

Chapter 6: The Paradox

1. James Strong, Strong's Exhaustive Concordance of the Bible, s.v. "workmanship," BibleStudyTools.com, accessed October 20, 2018, https://www.biblestudytools.com/search/?q=workmanship&t=kjv&s=Bibles.

2. "How Michelangelo Painted the Sistine Chapel," Great Names in History, July 25, 2010, https://100falcons.wordpress.com/2010/07/25/how-michelangelo-painted-the-sistine-chapel/.

3. New World Encyclopedia, s.v. "Sistine Chapel," last modified September 22, 2015, http://www.newworldencyclopedia.org/entry/Sistine_Chapel.

4. Merriam-Webster, s.v. "calamity (n.)," accessed October 15, 2018, http://www.merriam-webster.com/dictionary/calamity.

Chapter 7: The Bible Doesn't Tell You That!

1. Merriam-Webster, s.v. "kindness (n.)," accessed October 15, 2018, http://www.merriam-webster.com/dictionary/kindness.

Chapter 8: Resting in the Power

1. "Boston," SheKnows, accessed April 24, 2019, https://www.sheknows.com/baby-names/name/boston/. Also, "Matthew," Behind the Name, updated May 31, 2018, https://www.behindthename.com/name/matthew.

2. We originally started receiving pastoral input on our decision to move from the elder who developed ALS, it was after his diagnosis that we transitioned to receiving pastoral guidance from another pastoral couple who supported me during my years of Bible college.

About the Author

Stephanie is a millennial and a grown-up pastor's kid who cares about healthy church leaders and families. She grew up in Boise, Idaho, graduated from Portland Bible College and serves alongside her husband, as a staff pastor at Manna-house (formerly known as City Bible Church) in Portland, Oregon. Stephanie is a mom of two boys, a six wing seven on the enneagram, loves coffee and authentic Mexican food.

For more by Stephanie, including a free *Read the Book* printable workbook, visit www.andersonswife.com/rtbworkbook

Workbook includes:
- Chasing a dream (chart)
- How to hear God (workshop)
- How to study a topic in the Bible (worksheet)
- Effective living (interview)
- How to invite a friend to church (script)
- How to evangelize (script) … and more!

Made in the USA
Columbia, SC
11 January 2020